A GUIDE to a Gı BARRIER ISLANE

Featuring Jekyll Island
with St. Simons and Sapelo Islands

and a Field Guide to Jekyll Island

Written by
TAYLOR SCHOETTLE

Illustrated by *Tylor Schoettle*
JENNIFER SMITH

Layout by
TAYLOR SCHOETTLE

Computer Graphics and Typesetting by
TOMMY JENKINS

Produced by
WATERMARKS PUBLISHING
ST. SIMONS ISLAND, GEORGIA

Printed by
DARIEN PRINTING AND GRAPHICS
DARIEN, GEORGIA

Library of Congress Catalog Card Number: 96-092782

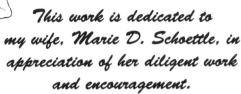

This work is dedicated to my wife, Marie D. Schoettle, in appreciation of her diligent work and encouragement.

ACKNOWLEDGMENTS

I would like to thank Kay Jenkins for her unfailing editing throughout the development of this manuscript. I want to thank my wife, Marie, for her editing and thoughtful suggestions. I would like to thank Dr. William Fritz, Professor of Geology, Georgia State University, for his assistance in the subjects of sedimentology and permitting my use of ideas adapted from illustrations in his text book (see Bibliography).

I would like again to thank Marie Schoettle whose steady hand made the final ink renderings of the maps in Figures 2, 3 and 4. Figures 1, 6, 9, 12, 13, 14 and 15 have been modified from the work of Charlotte Ingram and Carol Johnson in *A Field Guide to Jekyll Island*. The uninitialed plant and animal drawings in Appendices A and B are by Carol Johnson and were also transferred from the Jekyll island guide with permission of its publisher, the University of Georgia.

The illustration of the heron flying over the marsh on page 30, and the owl on the signpost on page 118 are drawings by Laurel McCook. The depiction of the Georgia Martyrs on page 49 is a drawing of a sculpture by Marjorie Lawrence. The illustration of the British troops on page 50 is a drawing from a photograph by Tommy Jenkins. The illustrations of Cannon's Point, on page 53, and the slave cabin below are drawings of photographs by Peggy Buchan, whose husband manages Taylor's Fish Camp on St. Simons Island.

Slave cabin at Taylor's Fish Camp (Peggy's Studio)

TABLE OF CONTENTS

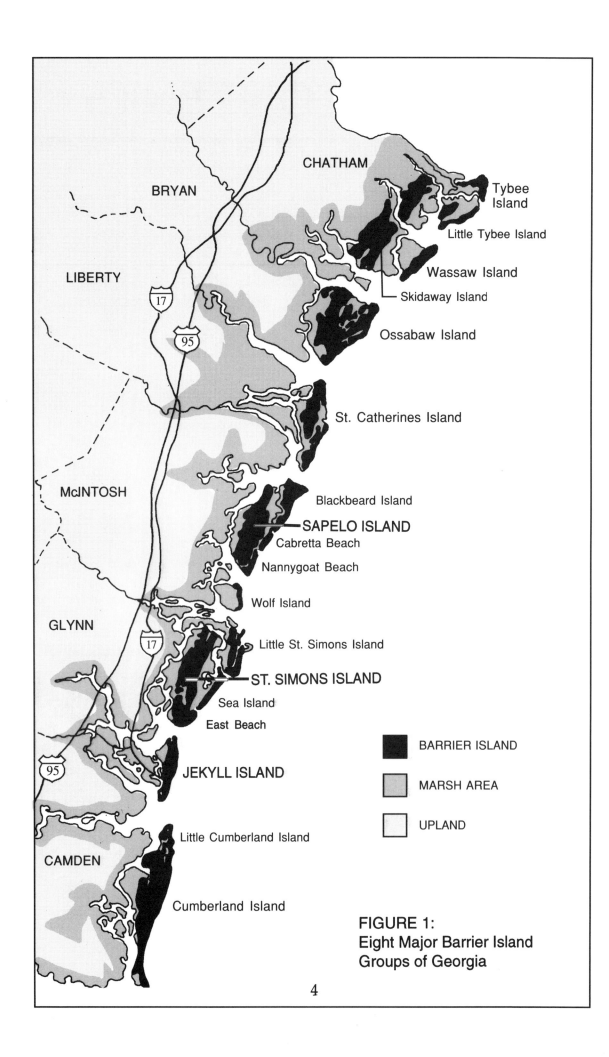

CHATHAM

BRYAN

Tybee Island

Little Tybee Island

Wassaw Island

Skidaway Island

LIBERTY

17

95

Ossabaw Island

St. Catherines Island

McINTOSH

Blackbeard Island

SAPELO ISLAND

Cabretta Beach

Nannygoat Beach

Wolf Island

GLYNN

17

Little St. Simons Island

ST. SIMONS ISLAND

Sea Island

East Beach

95

JEKYLL ISLAND

BARRIER ISLAND

MARSH AREA

UPLAND

Little Cumberland Island

CAMDEN

Cumberland Island

FIGURE 1:
Eight Major Barrier Island
Groups of Georgia

4

INTRODUCTION

Along the coast of Georgia, eight clusters of barrier islands are separated from the mainland by an extensive system of salt marshes and sounds (see Figure 1). Barrier islands form most of the beaches of the Atlantic and Gulf states. The term "barrier" refers to the protective role the islands and their marshes play in shielding the mainland from oceanic storms.

Unlike many of the developed barrier islands of the east coast, the Georgia barrier islands still retain much of their native wilderness. Approximately two-thirds of the islands are designated as parks, wildlife refuges, research reserves, and heritage preserves, with limited or no public access.

The four barrier islands accessible by causeway are Jekyll Island, St. Simons Island, Sea Island and Tybee Island. Of the four islands, Jekyll has by far the most area preserved in a natural state. Its long history of private ownership and management as a state park has been largely responsible for the island's natural preservation today. For this reason and the fact that the island is accessible by a causeway, Jekyll Island has been chosen to be the main prototype for this guide.

Examples of natural and human history are also drawn from the islands of St. Simons and Sapelo. The comparisons of these three islands along with examples from the other barrier islands will give the reader an appreciation of the similarities in the overall features and movement patterns of Georgia's barrier islands. Each island, however, has its own distinct version of the interaction of these elements. It is hoped that this guide can become a teacher and companion to anyone wanting to explore these serenely beautiful islands.

Taylor Schoettle
P.O. Box 1117
Darien, GA 31305
(912) 437-6799

PREFACE

This guide is divided into four sections. The first describes the physical setting, geology and ecological environments of the barrier islands of Georgia. Here, the geological history and physical forces that create the distinctive shapes, and dynamic changes of the Georgia barrier islands are disclosed. The ecological features that characterize the ocean beaches, salt marshes, maritime forests, and sloughs are described. Although these subjects apply to all of Georgia's barrier islands, Jekyll, St. Simons and Sapelo Islands are often referred to as examples. Included in this section is a comparative look at the human history of these three islands. This section is a brief outline of the history for the primary purpose of better understanding the impact of human influence on the natural environments of these islands.

The second section outlines the field trip to Jekyll Island and presents the sites to be visited. The sites not only detail each of the designated areas of Jekyll but provide examples of the general phenomena described in the first section. Frequent cross-referencing of related information occurs among these two sections and the Glossary.

The third section is the Glossary of Terms and Concepts. For quick reference, the upper right page corners of this section are marked. This section offers definitions and explanations of the technical terms used in the text which are designated by *italics*. Some terms require only a short definition while others, which introduce concepts, may require several paragraphs with figures. Terms in one area of the Glossary often interrelate with terms from other areas, fostering the integration of concepts and occasionally spawning new perspectives. In this way the Glossary has become an instructional entity in itself. For educa-

tors, efforts have been made to include terms that are taken from basic science curricula, so that students can appreciate how terms and concepts learned in school are applied to subjects involving the coast. Since the definitions and explanations in the Glossary serve to clarify the meaning of terms as used in the text, they may vary somewhat from those employed in standard textbooks.

Appendices comprise the fourth section. Appendix A is a guide to the identification of the common plants found in the various ecological settings of barrier islands. Appendix B identifies the living animals most frequently found on barrier beaches and marshes. Appendix C is a list of recommended books and field guides. Appendix D is a bibliography. Appendix E is a section on Personal Safety.

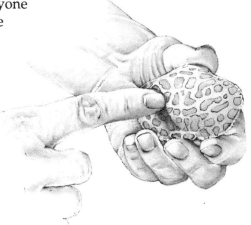

This publication is intended for anyone interested in learning more about the natural history of Georgia's barrier islands. The book is designed to be read on two levels. Similar to my previous guides, the text of this book submits information on the basis of what is perceived in the descriptions, maps and figures in the text, and from what is observed in the field. With little or no reference to the Glossary, this book is highly informative and enjoyable. The second level combines the text with a more extensive use of the Glossary which avails to the reader more theory, related concepts, and comparisons which enhance understanding and expand the scope of the text. This second track is designed for naturalists, educators, and those with a deeper interest in the subject. The Glossary, however, is there for any reader to pursue particular subjects that pique interest.

It is hoped that this guide will encourage educators to visit the coast with their students and will facilitate their preparation of study materials. Academically, the language and content of this book targets high school and undergraduate college levels, but by no means excludes an inspired middle school teacher and class from making effective use of this guide. By becoming better informed on the nature and dynamics of barrier islands, we and future generations will be able to make better decisions on maintaining a healthy coastal environment and preserving these serenely beautiful islands.

Lichens

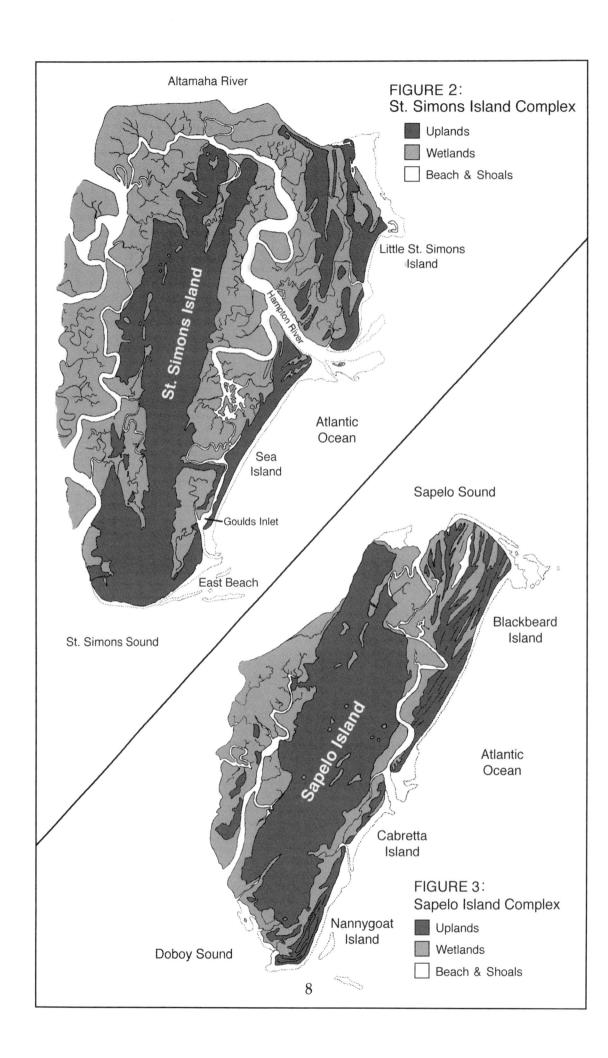

Altamaha River

FIGURE 2:
St. Simons Island Complex

Uplands
Wetlands
Beach & Shoals

Little St. Simons
Island

St. Simons Island

Hampton River

Atlantic
Ocean

Sea
Island

Goulds Inlet

East Beach

St. Simons Sound

Sapelo Sound

Blackbeard
Island

Sapelo Island

Atlantic
Ocean

Cabretta
Island

FIGURE 3:
Sapelo Island Complex

Uplands
Wetlands
Beach & Shoals

Nannygoat
Island

Doboy Sound

8

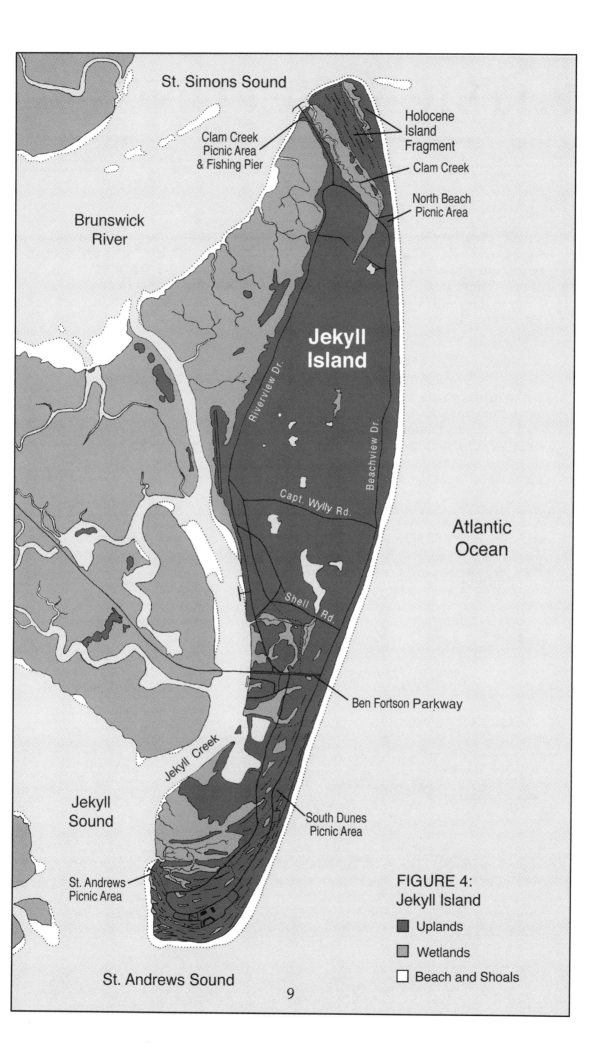

St. Simons Sound

Clam Creek
Picnic Area
& Fishing Pier

Holocene
Island
Fragment

Clam Creek

North Beach
Picnic Area

Brunswick
River

**Jekyll
Island**

Riverview Dr.

Beachview Dr.

Atlantic
Ocean

Capt. Wylly Rd.

Shell Rd

Ben Fortson Parkway

Jekyll Creek

Jekyll
Sound

South Dunes
Picnic Area

St. Andrews
Picnic Area

FIGURE 4:
Jekyll Island

◼ Uplands

▦ Wetlands

☐ Beach and Shoals

St. Andrews Sound

9

PHYSICAL SETTING

CLIMATE AND WEATHER

The climate of this coastal region is moderate, with short winters and long springs and falls. Temperatures during the warmest months (July and August) range from the 80s to the high 90s. From December to February, temperatures usually range from the high 40s to the low 70s, with occasional freezes. Because of the moderating effects of the ocean and sea breezes, temperatures on barrier islands tend to be less extreme than those on the coastal mainland. (See Glossary on *specific heat of water*.)

Average annual rainfall on the coastal islands ranges from 30 to 50 inches. During the summer months, a large *high-pressure cell*, called the *Bermuda high*, settles in the Southeast and is responsible for diverting large continental storms away from this area, with only occasional ones breaking through. (See Glossary for further information on the *Bermuda high's* effect on the local climate.) Most summer rains, then, come from local *convection storms*, described below. Sometimes these local storms fail to produce rain, and droughts may occur which may last for weeks and even months during the summer.

On a typical summer day, the air over the pine-covered mainland heats up and rises. These upward-moving air currents, called *convection currents*, pull moisture-laden air in from the oceans, creating the sea breezes which get stronger as the day progresses. The water-saturated air is carried up in the convections into the colder upper strata where it undergoes *condensation* to form clouds. Starting about noon, one can actually watch these clouds form and grow in the west as the day's heat intensifies. Toward the afternoon, great thunderheads migrate eastward often bringing short-lived squalls with pelting rain, a brief respite for a sun-baked land.

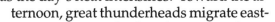

In the evenings, the earth cools quickly, disrupting the convection currents over the land. Because of its high *specific heat*, the water retains its elevated temperature, and the air over the water now rises a little faster than that over the cooled mainland. This reversal usually produces a gentle land breeze during the night (see Figure 5). In the morning the land breezes often go slack creating a glassy calm for a period of time as the land heats up. Once again the heat sets into motion the great convection generators ushering forth sea breezes for another day.

In late summer, the Bermuda high disintegrates allowing the coast to receive more rain from large, frontal systems. In the fall, tropical storms and hurricanes can bring the heaviest rainfalls. Northeasters, which occur in the late fall, winter and spring supply most of the rain for this area.

Prevailing winds are from the southwest and east in summer and from the north and northeast in winter. Hurricanes strike the Georgia coast about once every ten years. Hurricanes often follow the warm water of the Gulf Stream which flows close to the edge of the *continental slope*, about 80 miles off the Georgia coast. Looking at the map in Figure 6, one can appreciate how the extreme westward position of our shoreline often places it out of the path of hurricanes coming up the Atlantic coast. This westward position does not, however, protect us from hurricanes coming overland from the Gulf of Mexico.

Day (Sea Breezes) Night (Land Breezes)

FIGURE 5: Daily Cycle of Wind Circulation
(Modified from Fox, 1983)[1]

TIDES AND WAVES

Typical of tidal patterns along the southeastern coast, Georgia has *semidiurnal tides* or two high tides and two low tides each day. (See *tides* in the Glossary for an explanation of the forces creating semidiurnal tides.) The range of Georgia tides, however, is not typical. While Cape Hatteras, to the north, has 2- to 3-foot tides and Miami, to the south, has 1- to 2-foot tides, the Georgia coast has 6- to 9-foot tides.

Figure 6 shows that the coast of Georgia is the most westward location of the Atlantic seaboard. It is in the approximate center of the inward-curving coastline known as the South Atlantic Bight, which extends from Cape Hatteras, North Carolina, to Miami, Florida. The offshore tidal range of the Atlantic Ocean is approximately 2 to 3 feet. Since the incoming tide reaches Cape Hatteras and Miami first, these areas receive tidal ranges that closely reflect those of the open ocean. As the water funnels into the bight, it piles up on itself creating a graded increase of the tidal ranges as one goes toward the center of the bight. Since St. Simons and Jekyll Islands are at the inward-most point of the bight, they receive the highest tidal range. The high tides and extremely gradual slope of Georgia's coastal plain allow tidal waters to penetrate deeply into the land, creating the most expansive marshes of the entire Atlantic coast.

Except under storm conditions, wave energy on the coast of Georgia is low. The energy of the large waves coming from the open ocean is dissipated by bottom friction as the waves move across the broad, shallow waters over the *continental shelf*. Offshore *sandbars* and inlet *shoals* cause further loss of wave energy by forcing the waves to break before reaching the beaches. Georgia's coast is more characterized by lower-energy, *spilling breakers* (see *breakers* in Glossary).

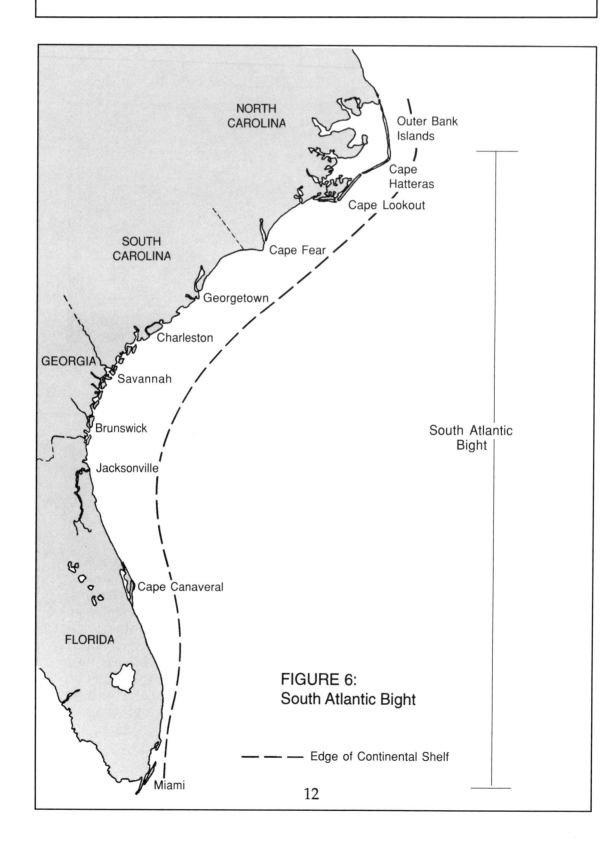

FIGURE 6:
South Atlantic Bight

— — — Edge of Continental Shelf

GEOLOGY

GEOLOGICAL HISTORY AND POSITIONING OF BARRIER ISLANDS

Figure 7 shows the three major topographic regions of Georgia. The entire coastal plain was ocean bottom as recently as 40 million years ago during the Oligocene Epoch and the fall line was the shore of that ancient ocean.[2] Today the coastal plain is mostly flat pine lands which cover the southeastern half of the state.

The *continental shelf* is the remaining submerged portion of the coastal plain. Glynn County's extreme westward position places our shore further away from the outer edge of the continental shelf (*continental slope*) than the other shorelines of the South Atlantic Bight. This places Glynn County's beaches 80 miles from the continental slope (see Figure 6). From Georgia's coast, the continental shelf declines very gradually, averaging 1 to 2 feet per mile. The continental slope is the actual edge of the continent whose slope rapidly falls to a deep plateau and eventually into the ocean depths, 2 miles down.

FIGURE 7:
Topographic Regions of Georgia

Over the past million or so years, from the *Pleistocene Epoch* to present, climatic changes have caused Georgia's shoreline to vacillate from the continental slope to 60 miles inland from our present shoreline. Seven sets of barrier island profiles have been identified over the 60-mile inland stretch (see Figure 8). The oldest and largest of these relic barrier islands is Trail Ridge in the Wicomico Island sequence. Its great size and position suggests that the island obstructed the drainage of the flat lands to its west when the sea level declined close to a million years ago. This obstruction contributed to the formation of the 700-square mile Okefenokee Swamp (see Figures 7 and 8), and diverted rivers on its western border to the Gulf of Mexico. The focus of this guide is, however, directed to the two sets of active barrier islands closest to the ocean.

Georgia's present-day barrier islands are actually a mid-portion of a system of sandy barriers which extend from the middle of the South Carolina coast to the mouth of the St. Johns River in Jacksonville, Florida (see Figure 6). The eight barrier island groups that skirt the Georgia coast are made up of two sets of islands formed during distinctly different geologic time periods (see Figure 9). The extremely gradual slope of the coastal plain coupled with the high tidal range of 6 to 9 feet creates the rare condition of tidal water completely

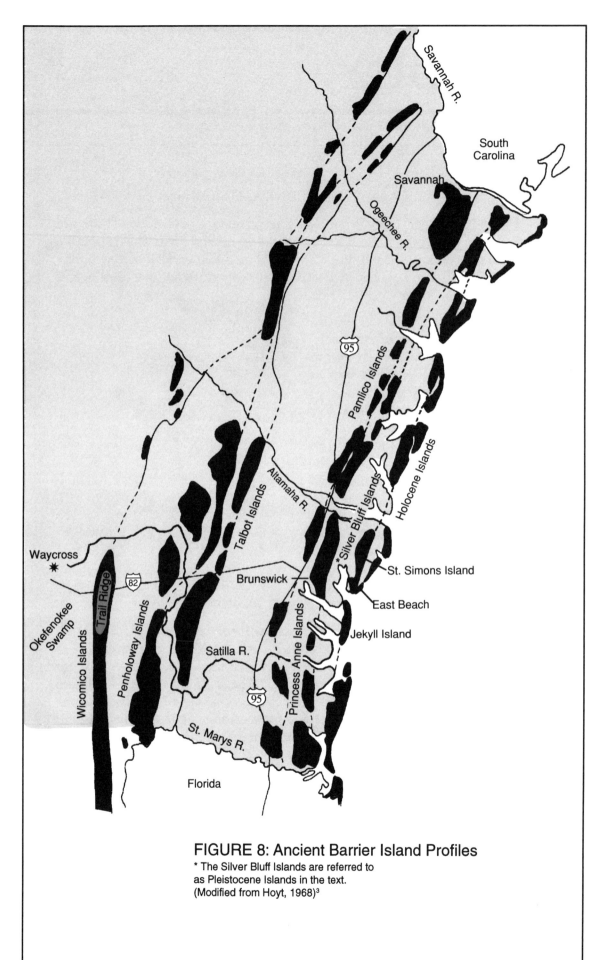

FIGURE 8: Ancient Barrier Island Profiles

* The Silver Bluff Islands are referred to
as Pleistocene Islands in the text.
(Modified from Hoyt, 1968)[3]

14

surrounding the older barrier islands immediately behind those fronting the ocean. In the majority of coasts, older sets of barrier islands become integrated into the mainland leaving only one set of barrier islands fronting the continent.

The older set of islands formed Georgia's beaches 35 to 40 thousand years ago, before the fourth and last great "Ice Age" during the late Pleistocene Epoch. Enough water was frozen during the last big freeze to lower the sea level 300 feet, exposing most of the continental shelf and placing the shoreline 50 to 60 miles offshore.

About 18 thousand years ago, at the beginning of the modern or *Holocene Epoch*, continental ice sheets began to melt and the sea level again rose. Sandy barrier islands near the shelf's edge rolled backward with the advancing sea level, migrating up the continental shelf. These rapidly migrating sea islands were narrow and were frequently overwashed by storms depositing sand on the back sides of the islands. Advancing seas also transported sand around the ends of the islands. Both of these processes built the islands from behind while eroding them from the front. In a phrase, islands migrated by "rolling over." Some of Georgia's smaller (Holocene) islands, such as Cabretta and Nannygoat Islands fronting Sapelo Island, show overwash areas that indicate active migration today (see Sapelo map, Figure 3).

Four to five thousand years ago, the rate of sea level rise greatly diminished, allowing the establishment and growth of the new islands in their approximate positions today. With the exception of Jekyll and Cumberland Islands, the Holocene islands form most of Georgia's beaches. Much of the Holocene formations which fronted Jekyll and Cumberland Islands has been lost to erosion, and the Pleistocene shorelines of these islands have again assumed those beaches (see Figure 9). The remains of the Holocene island on Jekyll is the small wedge-shaped mass of land east of the Clam Creek marsh (see Jekyll Island map, Figure 4). The remaining Holocene fragment of Cumberland Island, called Little Cumberland, is in a comparable location (see Figure 9).

Ancient terraces (large layers) of clay exposed on and just offshore of Jekyll's Pleistocene beaches are evidence that a stable Holocene island fronted the entire northern two-thirds of Jekyll. Clay deposits of that magnitude could not have accumulated on an ocean beach unless some land form fronted it and provided a shield against wave action (see Geology, page 18). One of these ancient clay terraces is seen in Site 9, page 94. Jekyll's Holocene island, at its greatest size, is believed to have extended from the northern tip of its present-day fragment to slightly below the area of Ben Fortson Parkway.[4]

The varied distances between the Holocene and Pleistocene islands often reflect the relative influences that the sedimentary outflow of Georgia's major rivers had on the inward migration of the Holocene islands. Notice the greater distances of Tybee, Wassaw, Little St. Simons, and Sea Islands from their Pleistocene counterparts in Figure 9. As you can see from the figure, these two groups of islands are immediately south of the two largest rivers in Georgia, the Savannah and Altamaha. Over the years, the copious outflow of sediments from these large rivers slowed the inward migration of these Holocene islands. Most of the other Holocene islands migrated closer and, in some cases, became attached to their Pleistocene counterparts because there was less sedimentary

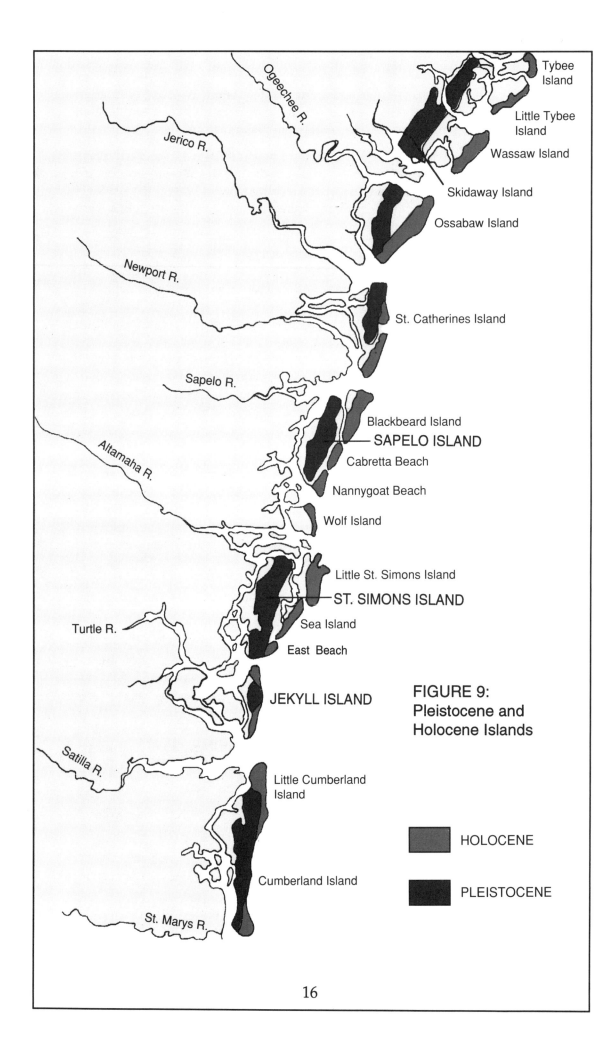

Tybee Island

Little Tybee Island

Wassaw Island

Skidaway Island

Ossabaw Island

St. Catherines Island

Blackbeard Island

SAPELO ISLAND

Cabretta Beach

Nannygoat Beach

Wolf Island

Little St. Simons Island

ST. SIMONS ISLAND

Sea Island

East Beach

JEKYLL ISLAND

Little Cumberland Island

Cumberland Island

Ogeechee R.

Jerico R.

Newport R.

Sapelo R.

Altamaha R.

Turtle R.

Satilla R.

St. Marys R.

FIGURE 9:
Pleistocene and
Holocene Islands

HOLOCENE

PLEISTOCENE

16

outflow from the smaller rivers to overcome. The fusion of East Beach (then a Holocene island) with the bottom of St. Simons Island and the southern ends of the two halves (islands) of Ossabaw are examples of such attachment.

Today the sea level is rising at a rate of 12 to 14 inches per century and its rate of rise is increasing. The Environmental Protection Agency and many other proponents believe that the increase in rate of sea level rise is due largely to increased levels of carbon dioxide and other *"greenhouse gases"* from the unrestrained use of fossil fuels (gasoline and other petroleum products).[5] In spite of the global sea level rise, the growth and erosion of our barrier beaches are more influenced by storm episodes, seasonal winds and tides, and shoreline engineering.

FORCES SHAPING BARRIER ISLANDS

The shapes and sizes of sandy barrier islands change constantly under the influence of winds, waves, and tidal currents. The ends of the islands are especially dynamic because of their proximity to the *inlets*. Generally, the southern ends of the islands tend to grow southward through *accretion* while the northern ends exhibit irregular growth alternated with erosion.

FIGURE 10: Form and Growth of a Recurved Spit

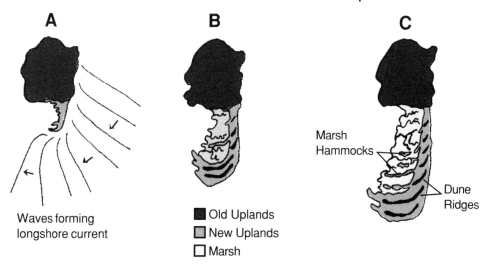

A

Waves forming longshore current

B

■ Old Uplands
□ New Uplands
□ Marsh

C

Marsh Hammocks

Dune Ridges

Southern Ends

Figure 10 diagrams the process of *recurved spit* formation through which the southern one-third of Jekyll Island and the southern parts of other barrier islands originally formed and grew. Water currents carry sand, which is deposited in shallow areas near barrier islands as *shoals* and *spits*. The diagram shows that spits continue to grow, *dune ridge* by dune ridge, toward the south, as *longshore currents* continue to deposit sand.

The free end of a spit tends to curve inward toward the back of the island; hence, the term recurved. As Figure 10 shows, waves refract as they approach the shore at an angle and turn toward the beach. When they reach the end of the spit, the *refraction* process curls the waves around the tip, creating the recurved shape.

The water on the west side of the growing recurved spit now becomes shielded from the surf, and suspended sediments tend to settle out of these quiet waters to form marshes. Jekyll Island, south of the Ben Fortson Parkway, shows classic land and marsh features which reflect their recurved-spit origin (see Jekyll map, Figure 4, page 9). The Study Sites of the South Area point out these features as they are encountered. Other good examples of land formed from recurved spits are the southern ends of Blackbeard Island, Nannygoat Island and Sea Island (see Figures 2 and 3, page 8).

Northern Ends

The northern ends of barrier islands show complex patterns of accretion and erosion which vary from island to island. Tidal currents moving in and out of inlets and longshore currents moving along the face of the islands often impede one another's flow causing suspended sand to fall out. This sedimentary sand is often elaborated into a series of shoals strung across the mouths of inlets (see Figure 11). Through southerly-directed longshore currents and wave refraction, the shoals tend to drift downward and inward toward the islands south of the inlets. Waves refracting around these inlet shoals create clockwise *eddy currents* which tend to hold up sand in the form of massive shoals close to the north-end beaches. The massive, north-end shoals of Sea Island, Blackbeard Island, Cumberland Island, and Wassaw Island are prime examples of this phenomenon (see St. Simons and Sapelo maps, page 8).

FIGURE 11: Inlet Shoal System

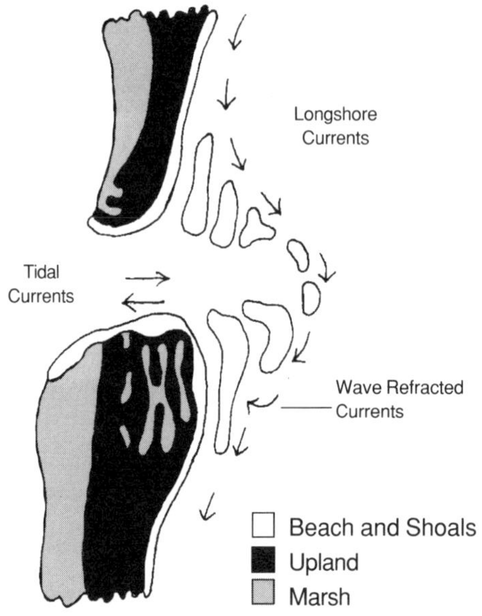

Longshore Currents

Tidal Currents

Wave Refracted Currents

☐ Beach and Shoals
■ Upland
▨ Marsh

Jekyll's north-end shoals are considerably diminished because of the St. Simons Sound ship channel. Most of the sand drifting down from Sea Island and the other islands to the north sinks into the ship channel leaving little sand for shoal development and nourishment of Jekyll's eroding northern beaches. (More on the effect of the ship channel on Jekyll's North End Beach is described in Site 8, page 89.)

18

Occasionally a nearby shoal attaches itself to the northern shore of a barrier island and establishes a new beachhead which shelters the old beach from wave action. The tidal waters remaining between the old shoreline and the new beach often become salt marsh, and may become freshwater lowland as the beach continues to grow wider and the area becomes remote from tidal activity. Any number of shoals may likewise become attached to an island, creating the often-seen corduroy pattern of *upland* ridges (old beach heads) interspersed with marshes and *lowlands* (see Figure 11). This form of "ridge and runnel growth" is responsible for the characteristic drumstick shapes of many of Georgia's Holocene islands. From their appearances in the maps, Jekyll's Holocene island fragment, Blackbeard, and Sea Island reflect this kind of growth.

Neither the accreted land on the northern ends of islands nor their associated shoals are very stable. During storms large areas of accreted land and shoals may become dislodged and transported with the longshore currents along the face of the island, nourishing the beaches with sand. In a smaller way, Goulds Inlet between St. Simons and Sea Island shows this phenomenon when it periodically shifts its tidal channel, freeing impounded shoal-sand to drift south and nourish the beaches of St. Simons Island.[6]

A COMPARISON OF THE SIZES AND SHAPES OF BARRIER ISLANDS AND INLETS OF GEORGIA AND NORTH CAROLINA

From the map in Figure 6, you see that the barrier islands of North Carolina (the Outer Banks) project out to sea and are located close to the *continental slope*. Here, the nearshore waters are deep, so that waves and tides reach these islands relatively unchanged from those of the open ocean. As a result, these islands have relatively weak tides and a high wave energy (see Physical Setting, page 11). During storms, recurved spits develop rapidly under the influence of large, powerful waves, often growing across and closing off inlets between the islands. The relatively weak tides moving through the inlets offer little resistance to the rapidly-growing recurved spits (see Figure 12). This tendency for inlet closure is the underlying cause for the islands of the Outer Banks being long, with few and narrow inlets. Occasionally (especially following a storm surge), new inlets are created when water rushes out of the sounds breaking through weak areas along these long, attenuated islands. The narrowness of the Outer Banks is due to erosion and overwash created by the massive waves that attack their shores.

FIGURE 12: Inlet Closure Through Recurved Spit Growth

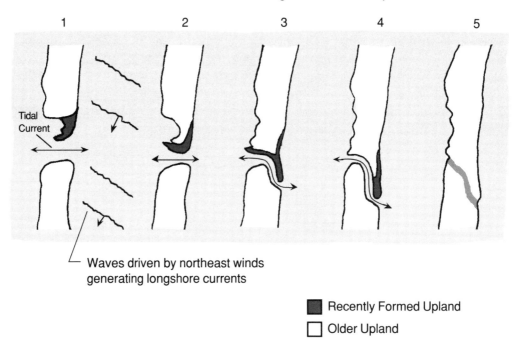

Waves driven by northeast winds
generating longshore currents

■ Recently Formed Upland
□ Older Upland

In contrast, the Georgia barrier islands tend to be short and somewhat wider. The Physical Setting section describes how the westward position of the Georgia barrier islands causes strong tidal currents and low wave energy. The strong tides moving back and forth through the inlets wear down the slowly developing recurved spits keeping the major inlets wide open and limiting length growth of the islands. With their lower wave energy, Georgia's islands do not have the wave attack that occurs on the Outer Banks and this allows for their greater width-growth potential.

In conclusion, the extreme difference in the distances of Georgia's and North Carolina's shorelines from the edge of the continental shelf has created diametric wave and tide conditions, which have caused the size and shape of the coastal islands and their inlets to become opposite extremes. As one travels between Cape Hatteras and Jekyll, the islands show graded changes in their features which range between the two extremes.

20

ECOLOGY

This section describes the four major barrier island ecosystems: ocean beach, salt marsh, maritime forest, and freshwater slough. Besides presenting a background on barrier island ecology, the descriptions in this section act as models for similar environments described in the Jekyll Island Field Guide section.

OCEAN BEACH

SAND MOVEMENT BETWEEN BEACH AND OFFSHORE SHOALS

Figure 13 is a profile of an accreting ocean beach which extends from the offshore *sand bar* to the edge of the maritime forest. The area between the sand bars and the beach is the *surf zone* where water moves back and forth in a conveyor-belt-like fashion between the breaking waves and the beaches (see *surf zone* in the Glossary for further details on the water circulation and sand bar formation). In Georgia, where the waves are usually small and the location of the surf zone constantly changes with the tides over a broad expanse of beach, the sand bars are not as clearly defined as those on higher energy beaches with smaller tidal ranges. The distribution of sand between the beaches and offshore sand bars and shoals changes dynamically with the turn of the seasons and storm episodes. This interchange of sand done through surf-zone transport is often referred to as the "sand sharing system," and is detailed in the next paragraph.

Strong onshore winds create high-energy waves which, when breaking on the beach, scour sand from the beach and dunes and deposit it on offshore bars and shoals. As the shoals build up, they cause the larger waves to break on them ("tripping" the waves) before they arrive on the beach. In this way the

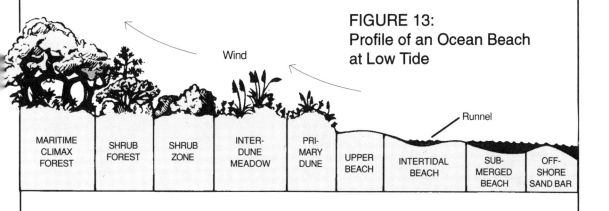

FIGURE 13:
Profile of an Ocean Beach
at Low Tide

Wind

Runnel

| MARITIME CLIMAX FOREST | SHRUB FOREST | SHRUB ZONE | INTER-DUNE MEADOW | PRI-MARY DUNE | UPPER BEACH | INTERTIDAL BEACH | SUB-MERGED BEACH | OFF-SHORE SAND BAR |

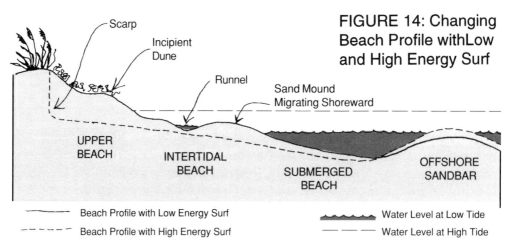

Scarp

Incipient
Dune

Runnel

Sand Mound
Migrating Shoreward

FIGURE 14: Changing
Beach Profile withLow
and High Energy Surf

UPPER
BEACH

INTERTIDAL
BEACH

SUBMERGED
BEACH

OFFSHORE
SANDBAR

——————— Beach Profile with Low Energy Surf

– – – – – – Beach Profile with High Energy Surf

∿∿∿∿ Water Level at Low Tide

— — — — Water Level at High Tide

breakers lose much of their energy by the time they break on the beach. The sand dunes and back-beach areas act as a sand reservoir which, when excavated by waves, releases more sand for further shoal development. The release of more sand into the swirling waters further wears down wave energy as the backwash drags the heavy, sand-laden water into the surf zone system. The sum of these effects works against sand loss and further lowering of the beach profile.

When surf energy is not as high, the action of the waves gradually transports shoal sand back onto the beach. *Runnels,* gullies roughly parallel to the surf line, often form where the shoreward-migrating sand moves up the wet, *intertidal* beach. Sea breezes blow intertidal sand, which has become sufficiently dry during the lower tides, to the back beach areas where it rebuilds the upper beach and dune systems. Figure14 diagrams the changing beach profiles described above.

Lettered Olive

The large continental storms, with their northeast winds, tend to erode the beaches in winter. The mild southerly winds and brief thundershowers allow beaches to build during the summer. Summer beaches are often characterized by low-lying, incipient dunes which form on the upper beach in front of the primary dunes. If the beach is accreting, the incipient dunes may become a new line of primary dunes; or, as is often the case, they are swept away by one of winter's many storms (hence, the name incipient).

Paradoxically, beaches, one of Earth's most dynamic and often dangerous environments, have become highly esteemed by people as places to live. Our insistence on erecting houses and hotels on or near ever-changing beaches has caused untold hardships and losses to us and to the beaches. The many attempts to save developed frontage and restore retreating beaches through the use of *seawalls, groins,* and *beach renourishment* projects have, more often than not, accelerated the loss of beaches. (The effects of these restoration methods on beaches are detailed in the Glossary.) More than a century of armoring and developing shorelines is seriously threatening the existence of natural, self-sustaining beaches in America.[7]

Mole Crab

ZONES OF THE OCEAN BEACH

Fecal Pellets

Ghost Shrimp

Intertidal Beach

The intertidal beach is the area of beach covered during high tide and exposed during the low (see figure 14). This area of beach usually has wet, hard-packed sand. Its width is regulated by the tidal cycle and varies with the slope of the beach. Because of the gradual slope and extreme tidal range, the intertidal beaches of Georgia can extend as much as a quarter of a mile out to sea. On the north end of islands, they may extend several miles offshore during low tide due to the inlet shoaling conditions (see Geology, page 18). The array of ripple forms on the wet sands of these intertidal areas are formed by the water flow and wave action and are studied in Site 3 and discussed in the Glossary under *ripples*. The aching feet resulting from walking over these expansive, sandy flats surfaced with hard, washboard-like ripples may become an incentive to find out more about ripples and their formation.

Few organisms can inhabit the intertidal zone because of the intermittent exposure to air and water, the constantly shifting sand, and the pounding surf. The majority of intertidal residents are found either in burrows or interspersed among wet sand grains. The holes of ghost shrimp and several kinds of polychaete worms can be seen on the lower intertidal beach during low tide. Ghost shrimp burrows can be identified by the short, rod-shaped fecal pellets surrounding the pencil-lead-sized burrows. People often comment how the shiny, fecal pellets appear remarkably similar to chocolate sprinkles -- the taste, however, promises disappointment. Impressions and trails of sand dollars, moonsnails, lettered olive shells, and other shallow-water, marine organisms can be seen in the lowest intertidal areas or shallow, water-filled depressions (tide pools). Upon seeing a circular depression with the five radial indentations, slip your hand under the pattern and you will bring up a living sand dollar.

Sand Dollar

Coquina clams, surf crabs and mole crabs, moving just beneath the surface of the sand, filter out tiny planktonic organisms suspended in the backwash of the waves breaking on the beach. Their presence is often given away by the little V-shaped patterns created by their tiny antennae or syphons penetrating the surface of the sand in the backwash. By quickly slipping your hand under such patterns you may be lucky enough to catch one of these animals. (The animals described throughout this section are illustrated in Appendix B.)

During certain seasons and weather conditions microscopic algae and diatoms living in the sand often produce green and mustard hues on the wet beach. Euglena are the algae often responsible for the green hues. These sensitive, mobile algae seek a certain intensity of sunlight to photosynthesize. On cloudy days, the green hues of the euglena are often seen on the sand surface. Full sunlight drives the algae below the surface so their presence is not detectable. On the occasion that sunlight is breaking through on a cloudy day and green algae is still exposed nearby, quickly position yourself so your shadow lies over the green beach. Stay as still as possible for several minutes. The algae, exposed to the sun, migrate below the surface of the sand, leaving behind the algae covered by your shadow. As you step back, you see your shadow momentarily left in the sand by the retreating algae. For the same reason the green color is often seen under beach towels, larger shells, and other debris left on the beach.

Euglena

The euglena and other algae are part of a world of tiny creatures living suspended in the water between wet sand grains, collectively referred to as *psammon*. The larger of the psammon, mostly amphipods and small polychaete worms, can be seen by flushing the wet sand through window screening or a household sieve. As the sand washes through with the seawater, the tiny wriggling creatures are left on the screen. These provide a principal food for the sandpipers that busily probe the sand with their beaks at the edge of the surf.

Psammon

Even though the intertidal beach is inhabited by a narrow diversity of resident species, it is a visiting place for a wide variety of aquatic and terrestrial life. Aquatic animals come in with the tide to feed and to escape from enemies. Those that die or are left stranded by the retreating tide provide food for the many shorebirds, ghost crabs, raccoons, rats, and insects that come from the land.

The presence of many small dead fish and other organisms washed up on the beach may be from shrimp boats working offshore. They take the shrimp and sometimes a few fish and crabs, which amounts to about 10% of their catch, and discard the rest. A trail of dead fish and crabs strewn along a beach is frequently the result of seiners who, all too often, have not taken the time to return the life back to the sea.

Georgia beaches have finer sand and fewer shells than most high-energy beaches. The coarser sand and larger shells are deposited on the offshore shoals as the energy of the incoming waves is dissipated over the shallow bottom. In contrast, high-energy beaches, like those of New Jersey and North Carolina consist of coarse-grained sand and broken shells which testify to the powerful waves that crash on their shores.

Shelling on Georgia's beaches greatly improves after storms and strong northeast winds, because the larger shells on the shelf bottom are scuttled up and tossed onto the beaches by the larger, wind-driven waves. With large storms, especially those associated with tropical depressions, our beaches are visited by a number of tropical species that are carried in from the Gulf Stream. Rafts of Sargassum weed crowd into our water ways and roll up in windrows on the beaches. Sargassum weed is a tropical, *pelagic*, golden-brown algae, kept afloat by many small spherical air sacs (see Salt Marsh, page 38 for a description of Sargassum's vital role as a safe-harbor for many animals in the open ocean). The decaying Sargassum on beaches emits a distinctive odor familiar to those who have lived close to the Sargassum-wracked beaches of Miami or the Caribbean Islands. This incongruous odor on our Georgia beaches is especially disorienting to me because I am instantly flooded with memories of past days living in Puerto Rico and St. Croix. Other more commonly-seen tropical visitors are the goose barnacles, with their striking white and golden-edged shells attached to floating debris, golden-colored sea hares (nudibranch), and the infamous Portuguese man-of-war.

Sargassum Weed

Goose Barnacles

The Upper Beach

The upper beach is the dry sandy area between the intertidal beach and the primary dunes (see Figure 13). In Georgia the upper beach is often eroded by storms or covered by *spring tides,* and it reappears during milder weather and *neap tides* (see Glossary, under *tides*).

Because of the extreme tidal range and gentle slope of the continental shelf, Georgia beaches are characterized by wide intertidal zones (wet beaches) and narrow or nonexistent upper beaches (dry beaches). Beaches with greater wave energy, steeper slope and smaller tides, such as those of New Jersey and Cape Hatteras, have narrower wet beaches and wider dry beaches.

Windrows of tidal *wrack* are often left along the high-tide line on the beach by retreating wave wash. The entangled stalks of the marsh wrack provide a moist, shaded environment for beach hoppers (amphipods), insects, and microorganisms. Such protected environments enable entrapped seeds and plant fragments to germinate and grow in an environment that would otherwise be inhospitable.

The cordgrass wrack also traps wind-blown sand, which begins the building process of a burgeoning, new (incipient) dune (see Glossary on the process of *sand dune* formation). Removal of sand from any young dune will reveal its cordgrass-wrack underpinnings. Pioneer plants like Russian thistle, sea rocket, orach, sea-purslane, and beach croton quickly occupy the incipient dunes and dry beach behind. (See Appendix A for plant identification.) The pristine, white flowers of the fiddle-leaf morning glory adorn the upper beach and primary dunes all summer long. As stated earlier, if the beach is accreting, these incipient dunes can grow and develop into primary dunes. Prior to understanding the important role of cordgrass wrack in building dunes, some of the hotels on St. Simons used to rake up the wrack because of its "unsightliness," and found that new dunes did not appear and beach growth diminished.

Fiddle-Leaf Morning Glory

The 1/2 - to 2-inch diameter holes seen in the dry sand of the upper beach and primary dunes are ghost crab burrows. Occasionally, ghost crabs can be seen out of their burrows during the day; but at night, the green eyes of hundreds of foraging ghost crabs glow from the marsh wrack in the beam of a flashlight. Ghost crabs are known as the "wolves" of the beach for they devour almost anything living or dead left by the tide. Ghost crabs impact the sea turtle

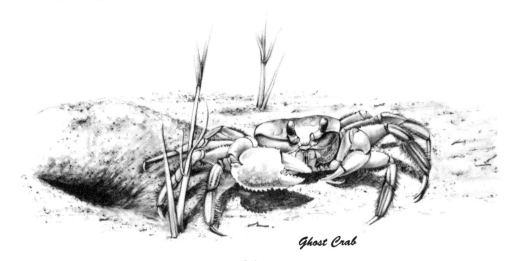

Ghost Crab

populations, by raiding their nests and by running down and devouring baby sea turtles as they scurry from dunes to the water. Anyone trying to catch a ghost crab will quickly discover why its genus name is Ocypode, which means fast foot.

Primary Dunes

Like the upper beach, primary dunes offer harsh living conditions because of the *desiccating* winds, salt spray, quick water drainage, shifting sand, and solar radiation. These areas are often considered the "deserts" of the beach. Many resident plants have developed adaptations similar to those of desert plants by having thick succulent leaves which store water and reduce surface evaporation. Yucca, a plant more closely associated with deserts, has deep taproots which penetrate to the ground water. Most of the other beach plants, like grasses, weeds, and shrubs, have extensive fibrous root systems which spread throughout the sand catching water as it quickly percolates through the sand. Root competition is stringent in these shifting, nutrient-poor, beach soils. A supplementary supply of plant nutrients comes from *inorganic salts* left on the ground surface by the seawater spray. The sodium chloride in the seawater, dangerous to plants, is diluted by the rains as it and the other more beneficial sea salts seep into the ground.

Sea Oats

On top of and between the primary dunes, grasses such as sea oats, salt meadow cordgrass, bitter panic grass, dropseed grass, and the aggravating sandspurs grow among beach elder, pennywort (dollarweed), beach croton, yucca, and prickly-pear cactus. Sea oats are the master dune builders. Their long curly leaves and tall oat heads trap wind-blown sand, burying themselves and neighboring plants. By growing vertical runners which produce daughter plants on the surface of the dune, sea oats stay ahead of the accumulating sand, while most of the other competing plants become buried, die, and eventually provide *humus* for the sea oats. This is why the tops of many dunes often have almost pure stands of sea oats growing on them. The lower illustration is a drawing of some of the scarped dunes in Site 5, page 80, showing the buried generations of sea oats connected by vertical runners to the daughter plants on the surface. Because of their vital role in building and stabilizing dunes, sea oats are protected by a law which imposes a stiff fine for anyone picking or otherwise damaging the plants.

Beach Meadows

Back from the primary dunes, the pioneering plants gradually yield to a variety of flowering weeds, grasses, and woody plants which make this area a beach meadow. Here, the beach soils have had sufficient time to accumulate *humus* with the passing generations of plant and animal communities. Humus increases the soil's ability to retain water and becomes a major source of plant fertilizer. These improved soil conditions have opened the way for the colonization of these highly competitive, dry-field plants. Such a progressive change in plant communities accompanying soil development is known as *succession*.

Butterfly Pea

The greatest variety of plants in the beach meadows is found in the *swales*, or areas between the dunes where the soil surface is better protected from wind and is closer to the ground water. For this reason these areas are often called interdune meadows. Camphor weed, wild bean, butterfly pea, pennywort, dune primrose, spurge-nettle, muhley grass, and brightly-colored firewheels occupy much of the flowering meadows.

The taller dune ridges of the beach meadows often continue to support sea oats and sparse communities of plants more typical of the primary dunes. Because of their higher elevation, the dune-ridge communities are exposed to salt-laden winds which severely desiccate plant tissues. Soil development is retarded by winds blowing away most of the dead plant and animal materials accumulating on the surface of the dunes. Poor water retention and remoteness from the ground water keep the dune soils dry. Soil development on dunes is sufficiently retarded that it is not uncommon to have sea oat-

Muhley Grass

covered dune ridges in shrub zones and in forested areas well behind the beach. An example of this is seen in Site 3, page 70. Most beaches that have been actively accreting over the years have broad, well-developed beach meadows, as seen in beaches close to the southern end of Jekyll Island (Sites 3, 4, and 5).

Shrubs and Forests

As the beach soils continue to age and develop, wax myrtles are usually the first woody shrubs to appear in the swales among meadow weeds and grasses. As wax myrtles proliferate and grow, they eventually shade out most of the sun-loving meadow plants which sets into motion a succession leading to a shrub zone. In the rapidly growing beaches of Jekyll's south end, pure stands of wax myrtles appear behind the beach meadows. From there they continue to grow rapidly and, with the arrival of other woody plants, eventually succeed to a shrub forest.

Cat Brier

On drier beaches, such as those on the southern spit of Sea Island, the wax myrtles are often dwarfed and entangled with cat brier, pepper vine, Virginia creeper, muscadine grape, and other woody vines to become shrubby thickets.[8] Having poor water retention and lacking nutrients in the soils, these dry, wind-blown, shrub thickets are slow to succeed beyond this point and often remain in this condition for many years.

With the passage of time and further soil development, trees, such as pine, yaupon holly, red cedar, groundsel-tree, red-bay, Hercules' club, and a variety of hybrid oaks, and the woody vines mentioned above join the fully-developed wax myrtles, transforming the area into a shrub forest. Unlike the maritime forest, the shrub forest lacks a clearly defined *canopy*.

Cardinal

These ragged, vine-entangled, shrub forests are a sanctuary for much of the wildlife of the barrier island. The soft staccato "check" sounds which accompany the nervous movements of the yellow-rumped warblers permeate these low woods and myrtled shrub zones in winter. In spring, the warbler's sounds are joined by the bright patterned songs of the cardinal and the soft breezy whistles of the rufous-sided towhee.

Further back, live oaks become established and grow. Eventually they, along with the pines and woody vines, form a forest canopy which shades out many of the shrub forest plants. Some of the wax myrtles, cedars, red bays and hollies survive to become understory species of the developing maritime forest. Under the best conditions, it takes up to a century for a beach to develop soil that can support a maritime forest.

Wax Myrtle

Beaches that are eroding often lack dunes and meadows, and have shrubs and even forests in the wave wash. The advanced erosion of Jekyll's northern beaches have cut into the forests leaving dead trees laying on the sand, as described in Sites 8 and 9. With the global sea-level rise, such "bone-yard" beaches are a common sight in the northern-middle areas of many of Georgia's barrier islands.

The frequent association of this warbler with wax myrtles gave it the name of myrtle warbler. Because this bird frequents other environs, the name was recently changed to describe its year-round identifying feature, the appearance of the yellow patch on its rump during flight. Locals affectionately call them "butter-butts."

Yellow-rumped Warbler

29

SALT MARSH

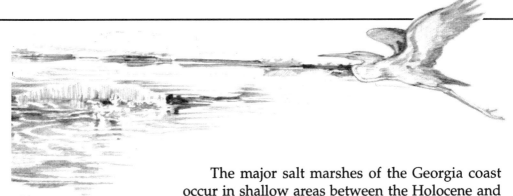

The major salt marshes of the Georgia coast occur in shallow areas between the Holocene and Pleistocene barrier islands and between the barrier islands and the mainland (see Figure 1). The marshes are flooded by tides twice daily. The large tidal range, together with the gentle slope of the continental shelf, contributes to the extensive, four- to eight-mile-wide marshes between the mainland and the barrier islands. The coast of Georgia is only 100 miles long, yet its one-half million acres of salt marsh constitute nearly one-third of all the salt marshes of the Eastern Atlantic States. The sheer breadth of these impressive marshes can be perceived from the various causeways to the barrier islands.

Marsh creeks, sounds, and inlets are all part of the *estuary*, where seawater meets and mixes with the freshwater from the coastal rivers and runoff from the surrounding uplands. The *salinity* of the seawater decreases as the water penetrates the interior of the estuaries. The daily overall salinity of the marsh and estuaries may fluctuate widely with the amount of rainfall and the height of the tides.

The marsh is a harsh environment for resident plants and animals. Intermittent exposure to air and saltwater, rapid changes of water temperature and salinity, and saturated anaerobic soils are among the adverse factors which severely limit the diversity of resident life of the marsh. The degree to which these and other limiting factors exist in the different zones of the marsh are explained in the following paragraphs.

FIGURE 15:
Profile of a Salt Marsh

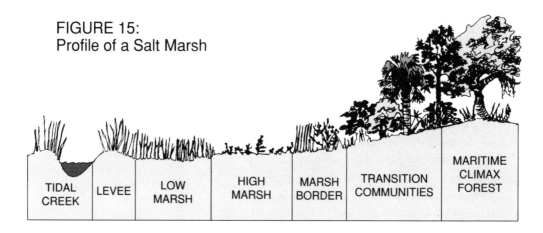

| TIDAL CREEK | LEVEE | LOW MARSH | HIGH MARSH | MARSH BORDER | TRANSITION COMMUNITIES | MARITIME CLIMAX FOREST |

30

ZONES OF THE SALT MARSH

The salt marsh can be divided into several ecological zones relative to the time and depth of tidal inundation (see Figure 15).

Levee Marsh

The levee marsh refers to the banks of tidal creeks. Relative to the other zones of the marsh, the levees offer the most optimal living conditions. The daily fluctuation in the salinity and temperature of the water in the tidal creeks is considerably less than that flowing in the shallower zones. The reasons for this will become clear in the descriptions of the low marsh. The constant agitation of the water running in the tidal creeks stirs atmospheric oxygen into the water, keeping it aerated. At a glance, the six-foot-high, smooth cordgrass growing on the creek banks attests to the superior living conditions of this zone.

Continual overflow of levees during the higher tides causes sediments to build up on the creek banks. Sometimes enough sediments accumulate on the surface of a creek bank to place it out of reach of the regular tidal circulation.

Halophytes on elevated area of levee

Under these conditions, the levee soils become dry with a high salt concentration due to evaporation. The smooth cordgrass dies and is replaced by glasswort and other low-lying, salt-tolerant plants (*halophytes*). Such plants are more typically found in and near a high marsh, which is essentially the type of *habitat* temporarily created on these levees. The elevated banks eventually dry up and crumble, and are washed away by the tides. Once again the levees are low enough to be kept moist by the tides and, in no time at all, they are again inhabited by cordgrass.[9]

Low Marsh

Behind the levees is the low marsh, which composes most of the southern marshlands. The incoming tidal water overflows the banks of numerous small creeks and floods the low marsh for several hours a day. As the shallow, *silt-laden* water moves slowly over the dark mud, it is heated by the sun. The elevated temperature increases the evaporation rate causing a rise in salinity and a decrease in the capacity of the water to hold dissolved oxygen. The oxygen is further reduced by the incessant, *slow oxidation* of the abundant *detritus* suspended in the water (see Glossary under *oxidation*). Aquatic organisms have to contend with these deminished living conditions. The smooth cordgrass only grows to about three feet.

Even the agents which contribute dissolved oxygen to the system diminish in their effectiveness as the water penetrates into the marsh. Tidal movement becomes sluggish and mixes less with the atmosphere. The oxygen produced

31

through photosynthesis by the algae, drifting with the water and living on the mud surface, is reduced because of the poor light penetration through the murky waters. In the oppressive heat, oxygen depletion can cause fish kills. Blue crabs have been observed to climb out of the water onto mud banks to breathe while awaiting a tidal change.

Blue Crab

At ebb tide, fresh water from Georgia's many rivers enters the marshes and mixes with the retreating tidal waters, which lowers salinity and brings in suspended sediments, nutrients and riverine life. The degree of salinity reduction varies markedly with the amount of rainfall and flooding of the rivers. Within minutes after the tide has ebbed, the marshes are once again inundated with sea water with its higher dissolved oxygen, increase in salinity and cooler temperature. (Experienced aquarium owners know how rapid salinity and temperature changes result in death and disease of fish – see Glossary under *osmosis*). Animals and plants, successfully residing in the low marsh, have evolved an amazing variety of adaptations to cope with the parade of changes in these vital factors accompanying the shifting tides.

Cordgrass

Killifish

Contrary to the limited diversity of resident life, there is a far greater variety of aquatic life forms drifting and swimming with the tidal currents. By moving with the tide water, these "visitors" do not experience the rapid changes in temperature, salinity and dissolved oxygen because they essentially stay with the same water as it moves through the marsh. Some visiting animals, such as dolphins, tarpon and cobia may remain in the marsh waters for a few days, while those using the marsh as a nursery ground may stay one or more seasons. More will be said about these drifters and swimmers being the key to the energy flow from the marsh to the oceans.

Periwinkle Snail

The mud of the levees and low marsh is well populated with resident mud fiddlers, marsh crabs (purple square-backed crabs, mud crabs (including stone crabs), oysters, ribbed mussels, polychaete worms, periwinkle snails, and two kinds of black marsh snails (the mud snail and the smaller coffee-bean snail). (See Appendix A.) The white periwinkle snails are seen moving up and down the grass stalks with the tide while they graze on plant tissue, algae and other attached organisms. Black marsh snails on the slick mud forage for algae and detritus left behind by the retreating tide, and the mussels filter-feed with the tide's return.

Ribbed Mussels

32

High Marsh

With a slight rise in elevation, the low marsh changes into a high marsh with sandier soil. The higher elevation allows this zone to be flooded by barely enough tidal water to cover its surface for an hour or less each day. The long periods of air exposure leave more time for evaporation, which further increases the salinity of the high-marsh soils. The high salt concentration severely limits plant growth. The cordgrass is either dwarfed (3 to 12 inches high) or not present. *Halophytes* such as glasswort, saltwort, and salt grass populate much of the high marsh. Often bare sandy areas, called "salt pans," are found where the salt concentration has become so high as to inhibit all plant life. Concentrations of salt more than four times that of seawater commonly occur in the *groundwater* of salt pans, and it is not uncommon to see salt crystals mixed among the surface sands.

As one moves from the low to the higher sandier marsh, mud fiddlers and marsh crabs give way to their counterparts, the sand fiddlers and wharf crabs (smaller, brown square-backed crabs), and the other animals of the lower marsh are either absent or only seen occasionally. The small (one-eighths inch) round, sandy pellets scattered about the numerous fiddler burrows are expectorated from the mouths of sand fiddlers after they have removed all of the algae and detritus with their highly-specialized mouth parts. The cleansing process usually leaves the pelleted sand whiter than the surrounding sand. The larger, darker pellets (one-half inch wide) are formed from sand excavated from the digging and repairing of burrows by the fiddlers. Sometimes the tiny black fecal pellets of the fiddlers can be seen, if they have not been carried away with the tide or covered with sediment.

Glasswort & Cordgrass

Sand Fiddler

At the approach of winter, the vast fields of cordgrass die and assume the tawny color of a wheat field ready for harvest. In spring, the emerging green shoots dislodge last year's dead stalks which are lifted up and carried off by the retreating tides. As the tidal creeks merge and empty into the sounds, the stalks of floating cordgrass pile up into large rafts. The rafts are carried to the ocean where they move along the shoreline with the longshore currents. Such

Raft Rider

rafts are often the vehicles on which insects, snakes, birds, opossums, armadillos and other land forms hitch-hike from island to island. The comically awkward appearance of long-legged egrets and herons riding these rafts in the back rivers never ceases to amuse onlookers. Much of the dead cordgrass ends up on the beaches as tidal *wrack,* and there it plays an important role in the building of sand dunes and in the growth of beaches (see Ocean Beach, page 26). We shall see how the decaying cordgrass is a major food source for the aquatic life of the marsh and surrounding nearshore waters in the coming section on the Vital Roles of the Marshes.

Marsh Border

At the borders, where marshes meet uplands, the ground elevation is above the high marsh, and the tidal flow no longer reaches this area, except during spring and storm tides. Without the daily wash of seawater, rains and freshwater runoff from nearby uplands greatly lower the salinity of the marsh border. The tall, dark needle rush and the yellow, aster flowers of sea oxeye in summer rim the marshes and hammocks, making the marsh borders visible from afar. In autumn, the light-purple blossoms of the marsh lavender and marsh aster add a delicate lavender hue to the marsh border. Where salt pans juxtapose marsh borders, the frantic, repeating call, "will-will-willet," may be heard in the spring and early summer. One or more male willets in courtship may be seen displaying their striking, black-and white-striped underwings, while hovering in mid air.

Courting Willets

Typical of many inter-island marshes with much freshwater influence, the entire marsh may be populated with needle rush. This is characteristic of some of the marshes in the middle of Jekyll Island, described in Site 6, and the marshes bordering Sea Island Road on St. Simons Island.[6]

Transition Communities

Marsh elder, a relative of the beach elder, is often found just above the high-tide line, giving it another name, high-tide bush. Groundsel trees grow on slightly higher ground behind the marsh elders. Salt meadow cordgrass, the predominant low-marsh plant of the New England and Middle Atlantic states, is a marsh-border and transitional-zone plant in the South. As its other name implies, salt meadow hay was (and to a lesser extent still is) harvested as cattle feed. The Ocean Beach section identifies salt meadow cordgrass as a resident of the sand dunes.

Cabbage palms are often seen at the edge of marshes. When present, their tall, column-like trunks are highly visible from a distance against the groundsel trees and elders. Further *Salt Meadow* toward the maritime forest red cedar, wax myrtle, *Cordgrass* yaupon holly, red bay, and the introduced saltcedar make up the upper part of the transition community (see History, page 55 for more on saltcedars).

Cabbage Palm

The same transition communities are seen surrounding the larger marsh hammocks which support maritime forests. Smaller hammocks may support only marsh border plants and some of the transition species depending on their size and elevation above the tide. These smaller hammocks are often named by the largest plant growing on them, giving them such names as needle rush hammock, cedar hammock, pine hammock, etc.

Where an upland rises steeply above a marsh, or where a shoreline has been eroded, there is little or no room for the transition community, so the maritime forest often extends to the edge of the marsh. The languid limbs of the great live oaks laden with Spanish moss, hanging over the edge of the marsh, create a serene setting unique to the salt marshes of the South.

MEANDERING TIDAL CREEKS

As one flies over the vast Georgia marshes, the array of contorted loops of the tidal creeks quickly becomes the center of attention. The mud and clay banks of the creeks offer little resistance to the erosion by the moving tidal waters. Because of the physics of water flow, tidal creeks are subject to the whimsy of *meandering*. Over the centuries, the never-ending, meandering process shapes and reshapes the loops of these tidal creeks causing them to take on their convoluted flow pattern, accompanied by *oxbow* formations (the Glossary, under *meandering*, describes and diagrams this process).

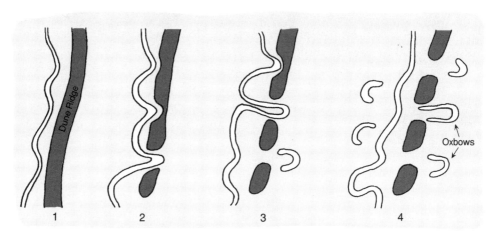

FIGURE 16: Erosion of Dune Ridges by a Meandering
Tidal Creek   (sequence over centuries of time)

Upland areas are never beyond the attack of the migrating, meandering loops of tidal creeks. Rows of tree-covered hammocks, seen skirting across marshes on the backside of barrier islands, are often remains of relic dune ridges, which over the centuries were cut into pieces by meandering creeks (see Figure 16). A dune ridge recently bisected by a meandering creek is seen in the marshes on the eastern side of St. Andrews Picnic Area (Site 4, page 77). Three meandering loops are currently encroaching on the narrow strip of land supporting Clam Creek Road (Site 7). A great area of the western shore of St. Simons Island has been removed by the meanderings of Dunbar Creek.

High bluffed uplands bordering marshes are often the tell-tale signs of erosion by a meandering creek. The "Guns on the River" display at Fort Frederica, on St. Simons Island describes the tactical genius of placing a fort on a bluff overlooking the outside bend of a large marsh river. Such placement made it impossible for oncoming war vessels to point their sideward-facing cannons at the fort before the boat was well within range of the fort's cannons. But, where as the fort may have escaped peril at the hands of man, much of the fort is falling into the meander it overlooks.

THE VITAL ROLE OF THE MARSHES AND SHALLOW SEAS TO OCEAN LIFE

Algae and smooth cordgrass are the main *producers* of *organic matter* and oxygen in the southern marshes. In the clearer, offshore waters, algae are the principal producers. As sea water penetrates the sounds and larger tidal creeks, it becomes more *turbid* with sediments, detritus, and suspended life as it mixes with the water of the marsh. In the marsh creeks, the turbidity of the water often filters out sufficient sunlight to prohibit photosynthesis just inches below the water surface. In these areas, the cordgrass accounts for most of the photosynthetic productivity.

Square-backed Crab

The cordgrass, as a living plant, offers little as a food source to the salt marsh community because of its high content of indigestible cellulose. Only a few animals such as the periwinkle snail, a few plant-eating insects, and the purple square-backed crab are able to digest cordgrass tissue. Smooth cordgrass is even a poor feed for cattle. After the cordgrass dies, however, fungi and bacteria, the principal *decomposers*, break down the cellulose in the plant tissues, liberating the plant nutrients to the myriad *consumers* of the marsh. The decomposers themselves are an important food source to the community.

Zooplankton

Besides the algae, much of the suspended life (*plankton*) moving in the tidal waters is composed of fragile microscopic animals called *zooplankton*. While some species remain as plankton throughout their lives, most are larval stages of every marine phyla, including commercial species, such as shrimp, blue crab, flounder, whiting, sea trout, and menhaden. The gray-brown, murky water of the marsh, replete with suspended life, is aptly described as a "vegetable soup." The *plankton* and small swimming life act as a self-sustaining "bouillabaisse" for the larger animals to feed upon and grow. As most of the larger swimming forms of the marsh grow and mature, they migrate to the offshore waters and become a vital part of the ocean's food chain. A seine net pulled in a marsh creek reveals a wide variety of smaller fish and invertebrates, many of which are immature (see list of commonly caught animals in seines in Site 5, page 79). From the preceding, it is clear that the salt marsh plays a major role as a nursery ground.

The scarcity of larger animals in marshes, sounds and nearshore waters limits the Georgia fishery to shrimp and blue crabs. A few other species, such as whelk (popularly but incorrectly called conch) and shad are harvested for short periods of time in the winter. At the turn of the century, oysters were Georgia's largest fishery, but outbreaks of oyster diseases have all but wiped out the industry. Quahog clams are plentiful but the labor-intensive method of hand-gathering the clams has limited this fishery.

Life in the open or *pelagic* ocean is spare and desert-like. Only in the top 100 to 300 feet of ocean is there sufficient sunlight to enable diatoms, dinoflagellates and other *phytoplankton* to photosynthesize. The pelagic oceans are on the average two miles deep. Most of the products of decay, which are the source of the algae's fertilizers, are located on the bottom. With thousands of feet of black water separating the photosynthesizers from their major source of fertilizer, the pelagic phytoplankton populations are kept to a stringent minimum. The algae are left to glean the trappings of fertilizer left behind as the dead organisms sink into obscurity. Since these planktonic algae are the main producers on which animal life is dependent, sea life as a whole is sparse in the open oceans. In temperate regions this sparseness of life is somewhat mitigated by decay products being brought up to the surface by *convection currents* responding to seasonal temperature changes. With these seasonal turnovers in the cold, oxygen-rich waters, the temperate seas harbor some of the world's greatest fishing grounds.

Phytoplankton

In the productive layers of the open ocean there is no land for animals to seek food or protection --the bottom is too far away. Many of the pelagic animals that are not large or fast-swimming, such as tuna and swordfish, or that lack other special survival strategies, often seek shelter in floating rafts of Sargassum weed. In the warm waters of the Gulf Stream and Caribbean these dense mats may exceed a mile in diameter and act as oases for thousands of animals that could not otherwise survive. Some animals are permanent residents of the Sargassum community while others, such as sea turtles, only spend part of their juvenile years there and move off at maturity.[10]

Sargassum Community

38

Windrows of Sargassum weed, blown in from the Gulf Stream, are sometimes found on our beaches after tropical storms (see Ocean Beach, page 25).

The shallower seas covering the continental shelves are the most productive environments of the ocean. In these *neretic* oceans, the bottom is sufficiently close to the sunlit waters to allow the algae free access to the decomposition products yielding plant nutrients. With unleashed algael growth and photosynthesis, animal life abounds in the shallow seas. Salt marshes, kelp forests, and coral reefs are the most productive of the neretic environments and are vital nursery grounds.

The diverse life in the oceans is totally dependent on the life-generating contributions of the neretic seas which surround the continents. These vital areas are also the most vulnerable to man's impact. Oil spills, industrial waste and residential development are escalating and polluting increasingly greater areas of these productive ocean environments every year. New earth-centered attitudes and far-reaching management strategies need to evolve soon, if we are to preserve the quality and diversity of life in the world's oceans.

Cormorants in the path of gathering thunderstorms in the western sky.

MARITIME FOREST

These low, dense, gray-green maritime forests cover most of the uplands of the barrier islands and are considered the islands' *climax community*. Other, less-stable communities such as beaches, marshes, shrub forests, pine forests, and freshwater wetlands tend to ultimately *succeed* to maritime forests, barring any natural or man-caused disruptions.

The larger trees of the maritime forest, such as live oaks, Southern magnolias, pines, and cabbage palms, intertwined by numerous woody vines, form the forest canopy. The canopy shades and shelters forest life and retains moisture in the forest soils. The atmosphere inside a forest is noticeably more humid than in the open. Shrubs and smaller trees, such as red bay, yaupon and American holly, sparkleberry, cherry-laurel, and wax myrtle form the understory. The canopy and understory provide abundant nesting sites and runways for birds, squirrels and other *arboreal* creatures. Saw palmettos, woods flowers, ferns, and younger generations of shrubs and trees form the ground cover. The never-ending shower of nuts, fruits, leaves, rotting bark and branches feed the wild animals of the forest and contribute to the accumulating litter on the forest floor.

It is surprising that maritime forests on the younger (Holocene) islands are supported by such nutrient-poor, sandy soils. The high humidity coupled with the long summers of 90-plus-degree temperatures facilitate rapid decay of the dead materials on the forest floor. In this way plant nutrients are continually released to replenish the soils. Most of the trees of the forest have shallow, wide-spreading root systems which quickly glean nutrients from the rain water as it percolates through the decaying leaf litter. Mycorrhiza, a *commensatistic* fungus, which grows on the delicate root tips (root hairs) of live oaks, greatly increases the root's surface area for absorption, as it takes in water and dissolved nutrients for itself and for the tree. Mycorrhiza associates with other plant species of the beach meadows and other areas with poor soils.[11]

For a few weeks in May and June, clusters of small cinnamon-colored orchids called coral-root *(Corallorhiza wisteriana)* grow among the live oak roots. Coral-root is a *saprophyte*, which means that it lives on decaying matter of the forest soil. Similar to indian pipe and other saprophytic plants, they lack chlorophyll, hence the absence of green pigment. The spotted, purple, downward-pointing lip of the flower helps in the orchid's identification.

The wide-spreading root systems of the oaks and other forest species interlock to form a dense thatch-work which serves to support the trees in the strongest of winds. An excellent view of a thick mat of entangled roots underlying a forest floor is seen on the North End Beach of Jekyll (Site 8) where a maritime forest is being undercut by erosion. Without their companions, single live oaks are susceptible to falling in high winds and they offer little resistance to the bulldozer.

Coral-root

If a maritime live oak forest is totally destroyed, centuries pass before the soil is again able to support another climax forest. Without the structure of the roots and the shelter of the trees, the thin layer of topsoil is easily carried off by winds and water. Without the trees and arboreal life to supply the soil with dead leaves, feces, and other organic fallout, the raw materials for building top soil are lost. Only the hardiest of weeds and grasses, similar to those found in beach meadows, can grow on these wastelands. From there begins the slow, tortuous process of plant succession leading to the eventual development of a maritime forest. A good example of a recovering wasteland is the Sea Circus site (Site 2, page 68). There a section of maritime forest was bulldozed, cleared, leveled, and left fallow for over 40 years.

Pine Bark

When fires burn live oak forests, loblolly and slash pines often take over, due to their rapid growth rate and ability to grow in poor, fire-cooked soils. Unlike oaks and other hardwoods, pine forests are unable to succeed themselves without frequent occurrence of fires or clear cutting by man. The young, sun-dependent pines cannot grow in the shade of the parent trees. Shade-tolerant hardwoods, however, do grow among the large pines and quietly "wait" for the great pines to fall from old age or disease, before they take over the canopy.

On the other hand, hardwoods are easily destroyed by fire, while pines have evolved extraordinary fire-resistant adaptations. Pines are insulated from the fire's heat by air trapped in their thick, loosely- layered bark. When the outer layers of the bark are burning, they curl and fall to the ground, carrying with them many of the hot embers that could otherwise damage the living tissues under the bark. An example of pine bark is pointed out in Site 4, page 75. When mature, the pines' 90- to 120-foot-high crowns are well out of reach of the flames of most forest fires in the southeast. In areas where fires are frequent, pine forests predominate and are sometimes referred to as "fire climaxes." Man often simulates the fire climax condition by setting controlled fires to cultivated pine forests to control the hardwood undergrowth.

Stands of old pines are often indicators of past farming activity. Again their fast growth and ability to tolerate poor soils allow the pines to take over the exhausted fields left fallow after years of intense cultivation. Pines make up much of the forests on the middle sections of Jekyll Island, most of Sapelo Island, and large sections of St. Simons Island where cotton was cultivated for more than a century.

Southern
Yellow Pine

The longer existence of the Pleistocene islands and coastal mainlands has allowed the time for better soil development than that of younger, Holocene islands. As a result, one finds, in addition to the forest species mentioned in the second paragraph on page 40, water oak, laurel oak, pignut hickory, red maple, tulip and sweetgum. The maritime forests on the northern two-thirds of Jekyll Island and the vast majority of forests on St. Simons and Sapelo Islands are growing on Pleistocene soils. It is not surprising that the plantations sites were chosen from these areas over a century ago.

Holocene forests cover the southern one-third of Jekyll Island below the Shell Road. Only a remnant of a Holocene forest remains on St. Simons Island, in and adjacent to Massengale Park. The Holocene forests of Sapelo are confined to the outer-lying islands of Nannygoat, Cabretta and Blackbeard.

LIVE OAKS

An old adage says that live oaks take a hundred years to grow, a hundred years to live, and a hundred years to die. Live oaks reach their greatest size between 200 and 300 years. Because of their stout, gnarled trunks and great, twisting boughs, most people overestimate the age of live oaks. They grow faster than most people realize. Edwin Stephens, who studied the growth of live oaks in Louisiana, said that a 30-year-old live oak may have a trunk two feet in diameter and most 100-year-old live oaks average trunk diameters of 5.5 feet.[12] The live oaks that line the driveway to the Sea Island Golf Club on St. Simons Island (Avenue of the Oaks) were planted in 1848-49, making them close to 150 years old.[6]

The Plantation Oak, located on the north side of the Crane Cottage in the Jekyll Island Club, is acclaimed to be the largest live oak on Jekyll. Its trunk diameter is 7 feet 3 inches, giving it a circumference of 23 feet. Its shortness of stature and robust health shed some doubt about the stated 112-foot height and estimated 350-year-age of the tree stated on the sign. The oak's lack of outstanding height is more than compensated for by its impressive girth and limb development -- a tree well worth visiting. The largest live oak in Georgia is 86 feet high, with a trunk diameter of 10 feet (31.4 feet in circumference). Its 143-foot-wide crown shades a full 1/2 acre of ground, and its appearance is similar to the large spreading oak illustrated on the next page. This giant is located in Baptist Village, Waycross.[13]

Wind-shorn live oaks

Growth patterns and sizes of live oaks vary with exposure to wind, sun, salt-spray, and quality of soil. The grand oaks seen from Riverview Drive on the northwestern half of Jekyll are tall, graceful, and of great mass, similar to those illustrated at the top of the page. These trees are sheltered from the ocean breezes and grow in rich Pleistocene soil. Compare these with the smaller, shrubbier live oaks on the ocean side that are dwarfed and contorted by salt-laden breezes. (Sites 2 and 9 take you to wind-shorn live oaks near the beaches, and the Glossary under *wind shearing, salt pruning* and *shrubbing effect* explain the interaction of sea breezes on the growth patterns of trees.)

Live oaks, *Quercus virginiana*, are confined mostly to the coastal plain areas of the southeastern Atlantic and Gulf states, from southern Virginia through eastern Texas and some occur on the west coast of Cuba. The leaf of the live oak and many other southern oaks are small and leathery with straight margins. Northerners are often surprised by the appearance of the southern oak leaves because they expect to see the lobed margins of the stereotyped "oak leaf" more typical of the northern oaks. The word "live" describes the fact that this species appears to retain its leaves throughout most of the year. Actually, live oaks drop their old leaves as new ones emerge usually in spring. However, residents living under live oaks are painfully aware that each oak appears to have its own time for dropping leaves making leaf raking a never–ending job. Raking might not be so bad if the small leathery leaves with the slightly curled edges wouldn't just bounce in place with each passage of the rake.

Live Oak

Ever since the middle 18th century man has ruthlessly cut down live oaks to clear whole islands for cotton plantations and to build the massive, live-oak warships, whose hulls consumed as many as 700 trees each (see History, page 50). Today the development of homes, condominiums, office complexes, shopping malls, and the widening of roads continue to consume live oaks. In the past decade, a growing appreciation of the beauty of live oaks and an awareness of their decreasing numbers is generating an intolerance towards their destruction. We are finally responding to the honor of having the live oak as Georgia's State Tree.

Live oaks growing in open areas produce wide-spreading crowns which often reach to the ground.

FRESHWATER SLOUGH

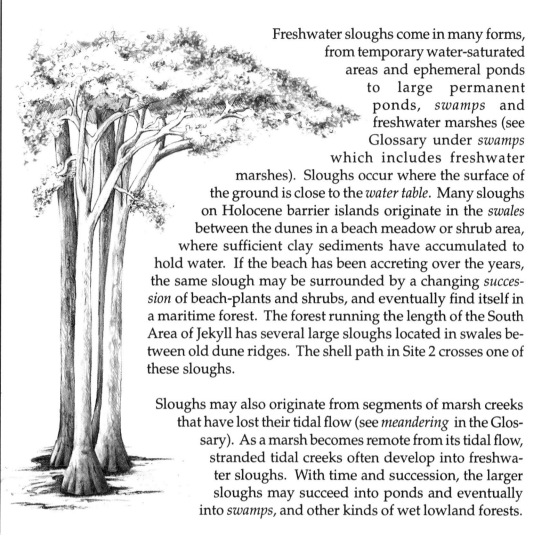

Freshwater sloughs come in many forms, from temporary water-saturated areas and ephemeral ponds to large permanent ponds, *swamps* and freshwater marshes (see Glossary under *swamps* which includes freshwater marshes). Sloughs occur where the surface of the ground is close to the *water table*. Many sloughs on Holocene barrier islands originate in the *swales* between the dunes in a beach meadow or shrub area, where sufficient clay sediments have accumulated to hold water. If the beach has been accreting over the years, the same slough may be surrounded by a changing *succession* of beach-plants and shrubs, and eventually find itself in a maritime forest. The forest running the length of the South Area of Jekyll has several large sloughs located in swales between old dune ridges. The shell path in Site 2 crosses one of these sloughs.

Sloughs may also originate from segments of marsh creeks that have lost their tidal flow (see *meandering* in the Glossary). As a marsh becomes remote from its tidal flow, stranded tidal creeks often develop into freshwater sloughs. With time and succession, the larger sloughs may succeed into ponds and eventually into *swamps*, and other kinds of wet lowland forests.

Hardwoods, such as red maple, tupelo, bay, button bush and water oak are variously represented in these watery forests on the barrier islands and mainland. Even from the window of a passing car, the presence of one of these lowland, hardwood forests is given away by the overly crowded stands of skinny trees. (A red maple - tupelo lowland forest is pointed out on Jekyll in the upper reaches of Clam Creek marsh, page 92.)

Many times the saturated soil conditions cause the hardwoods to buttress or to grow swellings at the base of their trunks, similar to the illustration. The buttressing is believed to aid both in the tree's support and in oxygen intake from the air, because the mud in which they grow is soft and *anaerobic*. To further increase air exposure, the roots of the cypress grow woody extensions, called cypress knees, whose knobby spires project above the ground and water surface in clusters around the base of the trees. With cypress trees and button bushes, buttressing is extensively developed with *fluting* to further increase surface area for oxygen absorption and for support (see illustration on page 47).

Mature cypress is seldom seen on St. Simons and Sapelo Islands because the few remaining stands are isolated to remote areas, and none, to my knowledge, occur on Jekyll. Extensive farming, landfilling and logging destroyed most of the cypress habitats. On the mainland, stands of young, second-growth cypress are commonplace along roadsides and parking areas that border wetlands.

Tree Frog

Sloughs are an important source of fresh water for the wildlife of a barrier island, especially during periods of drought. The deeper, shaded maritime-forest sloughs often have water long after other island sloughs have dried up, making them crucial freshwater reserves. Many of these larger sloughs were drained, the forest cleared, and the land leveled for agriculture during the Plantation Period (see History, Page 51). (Thus the maps of the Pleistocene uplands of St. Simons, Sapelo, and Jekyll Islands on page 8 and 9 are featureless relative to their Holocene counterparts.) Besides annihilating the cypress swamps, such drainage projects contributed to the destruction of many of the varied wetland forests on the islands.

Seasonal fluctuation of the water table in sloughs brings death to many water-dependent plants and animals. The accumulating dead organisms and moldering leaf litter build a rich humus in the slough and bordering upland soils. The greater incidences of drought in the past decade coupled with the loss of wetland habitats have exacerbated the scarcity of water for the islands' wildlife during the drier seasons.

Herons, egrets and bitterns often appear to be gazing over the water while fishing; however, due to the odd placement of their eyes, they are in fact peering downward into the water.

Sloughs add greatly to the diversity of island wildlife by providing a habitat for many forms of freshwater-dependent species, such as freshwater fish, amphibians, water snakes, the many insects whose life cycles require fresh water, and a host of aquatic plants. Sloughs are critical environments for Georgia's heron, egret, ibis, and wood stork rookeries. They provide nesting and feeding grounds for other waders, waterfowl, songbirds, and a variety of other animals. Because of the abundance of life surrounding sloughs, many larger predators such as alligators, cottonmouth moccasins, rattlesnakes, raccoons, opossums, and bobcats are also attracted. Alligators that have taken up residence in a slough often become "keepers of the hole" by digging out sloughs whose water level has dropped below the ground-level during droughts. As a result, groundwater is again exposed and, gratefully, made available to the other animals.

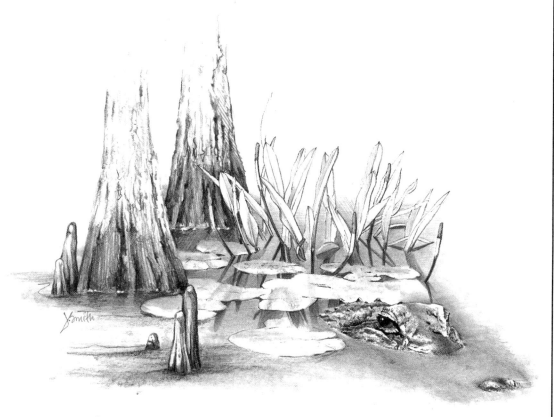

Keeper of the hole

In contrast to the quiet stillness of the salt marsh on a summer evening, the presence of a freshwater slough is broadcast by the cacophony of innumerable frogs, toads, and peepers.

HISTORY

The Georgia coast has a rich history. This section presents a brief outline of the history of Jekyll Island with comparisons to St. Simons and Sapelo Islands. Like three sisters, these juxtaposed islands passed through the same phases of history. At times two or all three sisters responded in similar ways, and at other times, they variously diverged; all three weaving their own destinies to arrive at distinctly different outcomes. This coverage is not intended to be thorough in a historical sense, but presents the flow of human events which occurred over the past 400 years. Through this historical flow, the influence of human activity on the islands' natural environments is examined. The history books listed in Appendix C present a more detailed coverage of the human history.

The three sister islands grew up together responding to the sovereign influences of nature and developing strong family ties and resemblances.

THE INDIANS OF COASTAL GEORGIA

The oldest remnant of Indian activity on the Georgia coast is the Sapelo Island shell ring which dates to 5,800 years ago.[14] The ring of oyster shells, taller than a man and almost the size of a football field, is believed to be an Indian kitchen midden (refuse pile). At the time of the Spanish discovery of the Georgia coast in 1540, the Creek Indians occupied the barrier islands and much of the coastal mainland. According to Edwin Green, the Creeks were tall and had a peaceful countenance.[15] They hunted, fished and cultivated corn, melons, squash, beans, tobacco and fruit. The large piles of oyster shells encountered on barrier islands testify to the Indians' appetite for oysters.

SPANISH MISSION PERIOD (1560 TO 1680)

While the Spanish occupied this part of the new world, great efforts were made to convert the Indians to Christianity and to take control of their lands and villages. Incompatible life-styles and beliefs between the Europeans and Indians led to much misunderstanding, strife, and martyrdom. Through the perseverance of the Spanish missionaries, the missions grew for 70 to 80 years. In the late 1590s, three missions were established on St. Simons Island and one on Aspo (Indian name for Jekyll Island) and a large mission on Zapala (Spanish name for Sapelo). Toward the end of the 1600s, Indian uprisings, pirate raids and disease led to the decline and eventual disappearance of the Indians and

The Georgia Martyrs

Franciscan Missionaries Martyred in 1597

Spanish missions in Georgia. Some of the unrest was spurred on by the British who infiltrated Georgia from their colony in Charleston, South Carolina. For a period of about 50 years, after the Spanish withdrew to Florida, a remnant population of Indians was all that remained on the barrier islands until the arrival of the English colonists.

THE BRITISH COLONIAL PERIOD (1730 TO 1780)

At the beginning of this period, the Spanish had a stronghold in Florida, and the British had colonies as far south as Charleston. The land between, which included the Georgia coast, was an area of ambiguous title and became the site of territorial conflict between the Spanish and British for more than a decade. In 1733 a British colony was established in Savannah, and, three years later, Ft. Frederica and Ft. St. Simons were settled on St. Simons Island under the leadership of James Oglethorpe. Shortly afterward, Oglethorpe had established a fortification on the north end of Aspo under the leadership of Major William Horton, and renamed the island Jekyll in honor of his friend, Sir Joseph Jekyll.

Major Horton constructed a two-story, tabby house and brewery. He planted 200 acres of English rye and 22 acres of hops to produce beer for the troops and residents on St. Simons. Ruins of these structures are found near the north end of Jekyll opposite the duBignon burial grounds on Riverview Drive (see North Area Site map, page 61).

Major Horton House

49

Three years after the British declared war on Spain in 1739, the Spanish arrived on St. Simons shores with 52 ships and more than 3,000 men. Edwin Green tells the most extraordinary account of how Oglethorpe with 630 men defeated and drove off the entire Spanish army and armada through cunning, bravery and discipline. The final defeat took place with the Battle of Bloody Marsh.[15] Retreating from Georgia, the Spanish set fire to Major Horton's house and outbuildings on Jekyll Island. The defeat of the Spanish sealed the fate that Georgia and the territories to the north would be of British heritage with English as their spoken language.

After the war, Oglethorpe returned to England and left Major Horton in charge of Jekyll Island. Major Horton rebuilt his house and remained there for the next four years before going to Savannah where he died. For the next 25 years, Jekyll Island and areas of St. Simons Island were owned by various British military personnel before they returned to their motherland at the onset of the Revolutionary War in 1776.

LIVE OAKING PERIOD (MID 1700 TO MID 1800)

Before the advent of metal-hulled ships, live oak was one of the world's most sought-after lumber for the building of warships for about a century encompassing the Revolutionary War. Live oak is a dense, heavy wood with many curves and a twisted grain. These qualities, coupled with the wood's resistance to rotting and weathering, made live oak vessels superior battleships.

Jack Coggins in his book, *Ships and Seamen of the American Revolution*, describes how trees whose great limbs took on the desired curves of various boat parts were carefully chosen and cut into large pieces. These were sent to ship builders where they were fashioned into massive ribs, bow stems, keels, knees, and other ship parts where curves and strength were required. The accompanying illustration diagrams how some of the boat parts were hewn from different parts of a tree. As you can see, the wood grain conforms to the curves of the boat parts, thus preventing their snapping due to splitting along the grain. The twisted grain of the live oak further maximizes strength. Live oak is so tough that shipwrights had to sharpen their cutting tools every 30 minutes when cutting the oak while the wood was green. Cured live oak was simply too tough to cut.[16]

Reports of British cannonballs bouncing off the hull of the U.S.S. Constitution, a live oak ship employed during the war of 1812, gave it the name of "Old Ironsides." These reports spread world-wide and set off such a demand for live oak from domestic and foreign markets that "live oaking" became a big business. Since 400 to 700 live oaks were required to build the frame of one of these great frigates, the barrier island forests of Georgia and Florida were ravaged. The live oak trade rapidly diminished in the middle 1800s with the increased difficulty in procuring live oak and with the inception of "ironclad" steam-powered ships.[17]

Beyond ship building there was limited use for such devilishly hard, heavy, curvaceous wood. Live oak was used for cannon carriages, wheel hubs and heavy wood supports like those used in the construction of the Brooklyn Bridge in 1886. The very properties esteemed for the building of warships are what make live oak undesirable as lumber today. The true value of the live oak is its magnificent beauty as a living tree.

PLANTATION PERIOD (1780 TO 1860)

For close to a century, the Georgia coast was intensely cultivated. Most of the cultivation on the barrier islands centered on cotton. The invention of the cotton gin, which eliminated the slow and laborious task of hand picking the seeds from the cotton, greatly increased cotton production. At this time the Industrial Revolution in England was mass-producing textiles by steam-powered mills. The increase of both supply and demand made cotton "king" in the south.

The Pleistocene barriers of Georgia were of special interest to cotton growers because the rich soil and sea breezes provided the necessary conditions for the successful cultivation of Sea Island cotton. Sea Island cotton was a highly-prized, long-fibered cotton that was imported from the Caribbean island of Anguilla in 1786.

In 1784 Richard Leake purchased Jekyll at a sheriff's sale and introduced Sea Island cotton to Jekyll which he cultivated for a number of years. Christophe Poulain duBignon bought Jekyll Island from the Leakes in 1794. duBignon was one of a number of French noblemen who came to America to escape the French Revolution of 1789. Prior to purchasing Jekyll, duBignon had formed a partnership called the Sapelo Company with two other Frenchmen and they had purchased Sapelo Island in 1790. Due to frequent feuds among the Frenchmen, Christophe left Sapelo and purchased Jekyll. duBignon established a sizable plantation which cultivated Sea Island cotton on most of the Pleistocene soil of Jekyll Island. Jekyll Island remained in the duBignon family for close to a century.[18]

Meanwhile, fourteen plantations scattered throughout St. Simons Island grew Sea Island cotton. Many locations on St Simons Island still retain their plantation names, such as Kelvin Grove, Retreat Plantation, Hampton Point and St. Clair.

Sapelo Island entered into the Plantation Period when Thomas Spalding purchased Sapelo from the Sapelo Company (the French partnership) in 1803 and established a sizable cotton and sugar cane plantation there. Spalding successfully introduced sugar cane to the Georgia barrier islands as an alternative cash crop to cotton. With so much cotton being produced at that time, a "glut" on cotton seemed imminent. Spalding's insight also included the modern concept of crop rotation to conserve nutrients in the soil.[18]

Sugar Cane

The grand life-style of these island plantations is legendary and is described in the history books listed in the Suggested Reading section. Edwin Green mentions that the era of the plantations started to decline sometime between 1825 to 1835.[15] The major factors that contributed to this decline began with the generation who inherited these beloved plantations. They lacked the fervor of the original owners and, in the face of hardships, looked elsewhere for opportunities. At a time when cotton production was peaking, both the demand and price of cotton declined (Spalding's prediction). England was having a recession and the docks were backed up with cotton bales. The plantation soils were becoming exhausted. (Cotton quickly drains the soil of its nutrients and most cotton growers did not practice soil conservation.) The destruction of cotton crops by the boll weevil became rampant.

This earlier method of extracting juice from sugar cane is still employed today in the rural South. "Cane grinding" to make syrup is often a festive occasion to bring together neighbors, family and friends.

National controversy about slave labor and new laws prohibiting importation of more slaves from Africa escalated both the purchase price of slaves and unrest on the plantations. It is interesting to note that the last shipment of slaves to the United States arrived on Jekyll's shores on the slave ship, "Wanderer," 50 years after the importation of slaves was prohibited.[15] The plantations could not operate without slaves. The Civil War, which destroyed many of the antebellum homes and properties and freed the slaves, brought the final blow to the already deteriorating plantations on all the barrier islands.

Cannons Point, St. Simons Island

After logging for ship timbers, lumbering, and clearing for cotton fields, most of the older trees of St. Simons Island, Sapelo Island and the older portions of Jekyll Island were cut down. Today, most of the forests in these areas are made up of pines and moderate-sized oaks and other hardwoods that have grown since the Civil War in 1865.

The South Area of Jekyll escaped cultivation and logging, as evidenced by the presence of its relic dune ridges and ancient, dwarfed live oaks. This area of Jekyll offered little for growers since it has the poor, sandy soil typical of its Holocene origin and a landscape rugulose with high dune ridges and deep watery sloughs. Even the live oaks were inferior for ship building because of their small stature and over-abundance of twisted limbs.

POST CIVIL WAR PERIOD (1865 TO 1880s)

During the Civil War, Federal forces burned and pillaged the plantations to the point at which they became inoperable. Owners fled and many plantations lay *fallow* for a number of years. Some of the former slaves on plantations remained and farmed for subsistence. Owners eventually returned to their devastated plantations and worked out loosely-organized share cropping and land-bartering arrangements with the former slaves. Attempts to reestablish antebellum cotton plantations met with failure under these working conditions. The boll weevil contributed to the failure and continued to suppress cotton growing until more modern means of pest control came about. Racking poverty, scarcity of food, political upheaval, disrepair of roads and railroads, outbreaks of yellow fever and malaria, and several severe hurricanes hobbled the plantations as they struggled

Slave Cabin

Chocolate Plantation, Sapelo Island

Sharecropper's Cabin

with their 'Reconstruction.' Such conditions created a fertile climate for the coming of wealthy entrepreneurs, attracted by the islands' wild beauty and looking for a heaven to fulfill their dreams. Others were attracted to the one resource still abundant on the coastal mainland and on some of the islands: lumber.

THE LUMBER MILL PERIOD (1870 TO 1900)

This period began with a growing international demand for Southern lumber. St. Simons Island and Doboy Island, a small marsh island south of Sapelo Island, became the ideal sites for the lumber mills because of their strategic locations on rivers. Cypress, pine, cedar and oak were cut from the flourishing mainland forests, and the logs were floated down the Altamaha and Satilla Rivers to the mills, where they were sawed into lumber for export. St. Simons and Doboy Sounds were full of great schooners from all parts of the world waiting to purchase the lumber. Sapelo Island residents made a thriving business raising cattle and selling beef to the captains and crews of the schooners.

This brief but bustling period closed with the depletion of the large trees suitable for lumber. A number of buildings in the Epworth Methodist Center remain from the mills that were located there on St. Simons Island. The Arthur J. Moore Museum at Epworth has exhibits and literature on the Lumber Mill Period.

Besides having a major impact on coastal mainland and island forests, more subtle effects on the environment accompanied the schooners. Before loading with lumber, the schooners had to dump their ballast stones. Ballast stones were carried in the holds of the empty vessels so the ships would ride lower and more stably on the open seas.

The piles of ballast stones were the foundation for many small hammocks, called "ballast islands", which appear in the Georgia marshes today. Three ballast islands are located across the Frederica River from the Epworth Center, and are visible to the left as one enters St. Simons Island on the Torras Causeway. A row of little ballast islands located near Doboy Island are visible to the south both from the ferry going to Sapelo and from the Sapelo Island dock.

Margaret Davis Cate described the non-native plants that grew on the piles of ballast rock dumped on the banks of the Frederica River. For this reason she called the ballast islands "Little Europe."[19] Tamarisk or saltcedar was one of the plants she described growing on the ballast islands.

Salt-cedar

Salt-cedar (tamarisk) has naturalized and spread throughout many of the marsh uplands in Glynn County. Salt-cedar derives its name from the plant's cedar-like appearance and affinity for water which it greedily takes up at the expense of the neighboring native plants. In this way, tamarisk tends to take over marsh hammocks and shorelines. From a distance, salt-cedars appear like pale, feathery, thinly-clad red cedars, and in summer, the hew of small pink flowers at their tops identifies them from a distance.

~

Jekyll Island did not participate in the lumber mill period because of the lack of suitable lumber surviving the plantation days, and because of the island's remote location from rivers where the logs were floated. While St. Simons and Sapelo Islands took part in the Lumber Mill Period, the duBignon property on Jekyll was divided and sold to a number of owners. John duBignon, a grandson of Christophe Poulain duBignon, shared a vision with his brother-in-law, Newton Finney, to make Jekyll Island a retreat for wealthy Northerners to escape winter's cold and to luxuriate in the balmy breezes of a Southern island paradise. While Newton Finney garnered interest in Jekyll Island from the members of New York's most exclusive society, the Union Club, John sought out all of Jekyll's remaining land owners and purchased their parcels. Jekyll Island was purchased in 1886 from John duBignon by a corporation of the nation's wealthiest millionaires, Jekyll Island Club.[20]

THE PERIOD OF PROSPERITY

This period encompassed the "Gay Nineties" and the "Roaring Twenties" – a time when money flowed, dreams came true, empires were built, and taxes were not a problem. Each of the three islands we have been following experienced its own version of this energetic and prosperous period.

One of the greatest expressions of this period took place on Jekyll while occupied by the Jekyll Island Club from 1886 to 1947. The dreams of John duBignon and Newton Finney for a Jekyll Island paradise were not only realized but far surpassed. With a membership that included names such as Morgan,

Jekyll Island Club

Carnegie, Pulitzer, Rockefeller, Macy, Goodyear, and other millionaires – "one-sixth of the world's wealth"– there were no limits to extravagance and exclusivity of the Jekyll Island Club. William and June McCash in their book, *The Jekyll Island Club*, detail the events that took place over these 61 years with photographs, documents and lively descriptions.[20]

From an ecological standpoint, the activities of the Jekyll Island Club had relatively little impact on the environment beyond what was already done to Jekyll during the Plantation Period. The goals of the membership were largely rest and recreation with opportunities for private discussion and making important decisions in a beautiful setting. With these goals, maintaining the island's natural beauty, and preserving the island's wild areas for hunting and fishing were priorities.

The stocking of non-indigenous game animals, such as pheasants and hogs, had little effect on Jekyll because their populations were kept low and were eventually eliminated through hunting. On other islands, however, feral hog populations have multiplied and their rooting habits and rapacious appetites have (and still are) damaging the forest understory. Fragile dune and beach meadow communities and vast numbers of sea turtle nests are destroyed by ravaging hogs rooting up and consuming the eggs. For the endangered sea turtles, such an impact, if allowed to continue, would exacerbate their already tenuous existance.

For more than 60 years, Jekyll Island was sheltered from rapid land-altering activities of agriculture and residential development that took place on Sapelo and St. Simons (respectively) over that period of time. The colony of cottages, social halls, stables, service buildings, nine-hole golf course, and playing fields of the Jekyll Island Club took up less than 10% of Jekyll's 4,012 acres of upland. The dwellings, being on the river side of the island, created little need for beach development and restoration projects. This particular time in Jekyll's history contributed greatly to the Island's preservation of its natural habitat.

~

56

From 1912 to 1953 Sapelo Island experienced its own version of an island paradise through the dreams and fortunes of two magnates, Howard Coffin, and later Richard J. Reynolds. Both men sunk millions into the reconstruction of Sapelo. Through their rebuilding and luxurious embellishments, the Big House (the old Spalding mansion) came to "rival any mansion on the

"The Big House"
(Modified from Sullivan)[18]

mainland." The lavish lifestyles of these men and their families attracted many dignitaries and two United States presidents to the Island. Over this period of time, Sapelo bustled with activity in its attempts to become a fully-operating plantation. Sapelo had one of the finest beef cattle operations in southeast Georgia and operated a canning factory for shrimp and oysters. Timbering also was a source of income for the island.[18] Today the preponderance of pine and second-growth hardwood forests and fields attest to Sapelo's extensive agrarian history.

~

Meanwhile, St.Simons, a public island with many owners, underwent its "Resort Period" with grand hotels, rental cottages and restaurants which attracted people from the major cities of Georgia and neighboring states. With the construction of the F. J. Torras Causeway in 1924, roads and summer cottages sprang up everywhere on St. Simons Island.

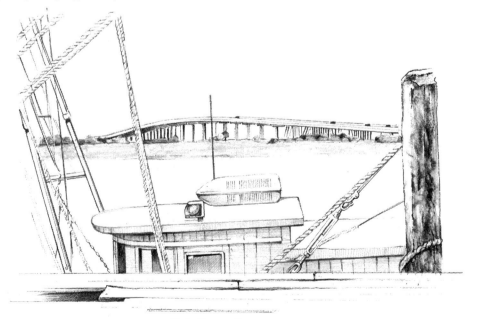

F. J. Torras Causeway

MODERN PERIOD

The prosperity of the "Gay Nineties" and the "Roaring Twenties" moved into the Depression of the thirties, the Second World War in the forties, and the advent of Federal Income tax. The fates of all three islands were inexorably changed.

By 1940 the Jekyll Island Club was experiencing escalating operating costs, increased taxes, and prohibitive expenses in its attempts to refurbish and modernize the antiquated Victorian facilities. Membership and enthusiasm were rapidly falling away with the death of charter members and the infeasibility of upholding the lofty ambiance of the past. Other attractive, less antiquated resorts lured away the membership. In its final years, accumulating debts, unpaid taxes and mortgages, and failure to comply with up-to-date codes and standards brought the island under condemnation. In 1947 the State of Georgia purchased the island for $675,000 to be appropriated as a state park.

Today Jekyll island is owned by the state and managed by the Jekyll Island Authority. Approximately 65% of Jekyll is preserved in a natural state which includes parks and picnic grounds. Of the remaining 35%, approximately one third has been developed into residences, hotels, and businesses where owners lease the land from the state. Jekyll is the only authority-governed park in Georgia where private citizens live year–round. The remaining parts of the developed island are golf courses, water parks, and other forms of commercial recreation.

Failing health, taxes, and prohibitive maintenance costs turned Richard Reynold's attention towards availing Sapelo Island for research, education and wildlife preservation. Over the next 30 years, portions of Sapelo were sequentially released to various divisions of the Department of Natural Resources and to the University of Georgia. Today the northern half of Sapelo has become the Richard J. Reynolds State Wildlife Refuge. A sizable chunk of the southern half of the island, including the marshlands of the Duplin River, has become the Sapelo Island National Estuarine Research Reserve; and Reynold's dairy barns, associated buildings and grounds have been converted into research laboratories, faculty residences, dormitory, and maintenance buildings of the University of Georgia Marine Institute. Over the past 30 years, the Marine Institute has been a world leader in research on salt marshes. A 434-acre tract of Sapelo known as Hog Hammock has remained in the ownership of the descendants of slaves from the Spalding plantation, and it is the only settlement of its kind, still in existence in Georgia.

Sapelo Island
National Estuarine Research Reserve

From the 1930s through the 1950s, many of the frequent visitors to St. Simons Island became residents. Houses were winterized, and what were once clusters of summer cottages became expanding neighborhoods, heralding in the present–day "Residential Period." The presence of the Navy during World War Two improved roads, the airport, water and sewerage systems, and housing which accelerated the post-war residential growth. Today, St. Simons is a rapidly-growing residential island with a rising trend in commerce and tourism.

EPILOGUE

The three sisters, closely juxtaposed, wove their way through history to become different: Jekyll, a state-owned resort island; Sapelo, a state wildlife refuge, a national estuarine reserve, and a research institute; and St. Simons, a residential island.

Through the avenues of time, the subtle differences between the three sister islands were variously emphasized under the economic influences of mankind, and now they play very different roles in a people's world.

FIELD GUIDE TO JEKYLL ISLAND

STUDY SITES

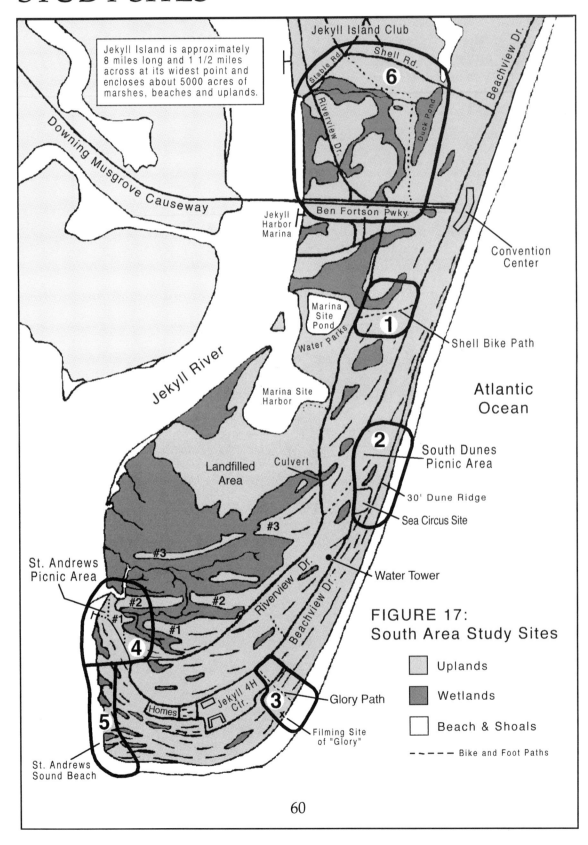

Jekyll Island is approximately 8 miles long and 1 1/2 miles across at its widest point and encloses about 5000 acres of marshes, beaches and uplands.

Jekyll Island Club

Shell Rd.

Stable Rd.

Beachview Dr.

6

Riverview Dr.

Duck Pond

Ben Fortson Pwky.

Jekyll Harbor Marina

Downing Musgrove Causeway

Convention Center

Marina Site Pond

Water Parks

1

Shell Bike Path

Jekyll River

Atlantic Ocean

Marina Site Harbor

Landfilled Area

Culvert

2

South Dunes Picnic Area

30' Dune Ridge

Sea Circus Site

#3

#3

St. Andrews Picnic Area

Riverview Dr.

Beachview Dr.

Water Tower

#2

#2

#1

#1

4

FIGURE 17:
South Area Study Sites

Jekyll 4H Ctr.

Glory Path

Homes

3

5

Filming Site of "Glory"

St. Andrews Sound Beach

	Uplands
	Wetlands
	Beach & Shoals

- - - - - Bike and Foot Paths

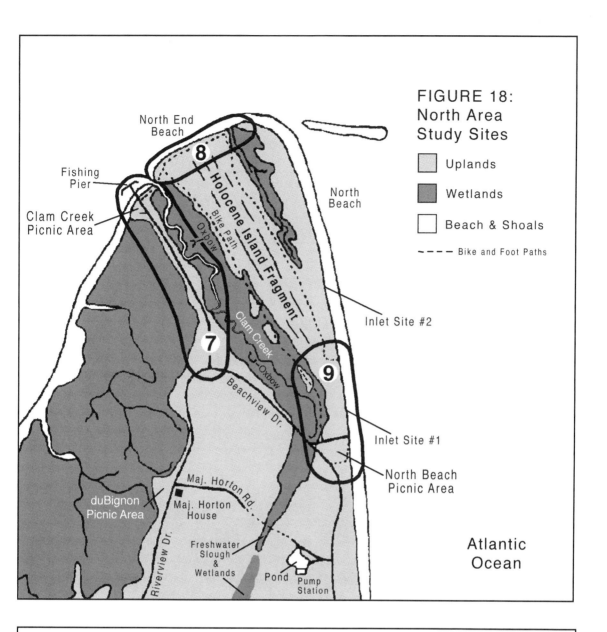

FIGURE 18:
North Area
Study Sites

Uplands
Wetlands
Beach & Shoals
– – – – Bike and Foot Paths

North End Beach
Fishing Pier
Clam Creek Picnic Area
North Beach
Holocene Island Fragment
Bike Path
Oxbow
Clam Creek
Oxbow
Beachview Dr.
Inlet Site #2
Inlet Site #1
North Beach Picnic Area
Maj. Horton Rd.
duBignon Picnic Area
Maj. Horton House
Riverview Dr.
Freshwater Slough & Wetlands
Pond
Pump Station
Atlantic Ocean

STUDY SITES

1. Shell Bike Path
2. South Dunes Picnic Area and Aquarama Site
3. Glory Path
4. St Andrews Picnic Area
5. St. Andrews Sound Beach
6. Mid-island Sloughs
7. Clam Creek Picnic Area and Fishing Pier
8. North End Beach
9. North Beach Picnic Area

Comments on the Study Sites:

Jekyll has been divided into North and South Areas because most of the study sites are located near the ends of the island. To increase the size of the Study Site maps, a middle section of Jekyll Island has been omitted.

The sites on page 61 have been arranged, beginning with the South Area and continuing through the North Area, to provide continuity of subject matter and to minimize travel. Visiting the sites in sequence is recommended because there is some information presented in previous sites that pertains to later sites. However visiting the sites out of sequence is feasible because of the frequent cross-referencing of information.

Although most people will be in automobiles, you may find that visiting the sites on a bicycle will add to your pleasure. The island is quite small, and most of the study sites in each area are fairly close together. The bike paths are excellent and bicycle rentals are available. (A suggestion for ease of riding: when traveling from one end of the island to the other, ride with the wind whenever possible, but when having to buck the wind, ride on the opposite side of the island from which the wind is blowing.)

SOUTH AREA

The South Area includes the lower one-third of Jekyll Island extending from Shell Road to the extreme southern shore of St. Andrews Sound.

The study sites and descriptions in this area appear sequentially proceeding south on Beachview Drive from the Ben Fortson Parkway to the southernmost point of the island. And then continue going north on Riverview Drive ending at Site 6 on Shell Road.

The 2 1/4-mile-long section of Jekyll Island below the Ben Fortson Parkway is relatively young (Holocene) land formed from *recurved spits* drifting down from the older sections of Jekyll to the north. The uplands that form this narrow strip of land are elaborated into relic dune ridges interspaced with *swales* oriented in a northeast to southwest direction. The orientation of the dune ridges is predictable in light of how recurved spits form (see Geology, page 17). As one proceeds southward, this area of the island becomes progressively younger until arrival at the southeastern tip of St. Andrews Sound Beach, where newly formed dunes may only be weeks old. The chronological sequence of dune ridges and swales makes the land formation of the South Area reminiscent of the growth rings in a tree.

With the exception of a few areas where the road veers toward or away from the beach, Beachview Drive tends to occupy a point somewhere between maritime and shrub forests. As you begin the southward journey from the Ben Fortson Parkway, the backward-slanting *shearline* of the trees on the right side of the road is clearly visible. Notice the severe shearing that has occurred in the wind-sculptured tree tops that have emerged above the protective canopy of the forest – see illustration at the top of the page. *Wind shearing* is further explored in Site 2.

SITE 1: Shell Bike Path

NATURAL HISTORY: A path traversing a young (Holocene) maritime forest from the ocean side to the marsh side of the island.

The shell bike path is a little more than 3/4 of a mile from the Ben Fortson Parkway. The entrance of the path is located on the west side of Beachview Drive just opposite the narrow, wooded border between the Ramada and Holiday Inn properties. The 2/10-mile path through the forest extends to Riverview Drive, just opposite the Summer Waves water park. There are several vehicle paths further south that traverse this forest, but these go through deeper sloughs that are more prone to be covered by water during the wet seasons.

From either Beachview or Riverview Drives there is no clue as to just how narrow this strip of forested upland actually is until you walk this or the other trails through the forest. Uplands formed from recurved spits are generally long and narrow as exemplified by the south ends of both Jekyll and Sea Islands (see maps on pages 8 and 9).

In the warmer seasons, carrying insect repellent is advised because of mosquitos, chiggers, and ticks (see Personal Safety, Appendix E). When walking on this or other forest paths, a twig is helpful in clearing away spider webs. The golden-silk spiders are most frequently encountered because their webs are sufficiently large to span across a path. Their webs *refract* a gold color when light strikes them, giving the web-spinners their name.

Golden-silk Spider

Anyone running into one of these large webs is immediately impressed by their strength. The orange-tan, spotted females can grow to an attention-getting two inches in length. Several slender, 1/4-inch-long males and occasionally a tiny parasitic spider with a round abdomen share the web with the female. Cohabitation of the web with such a formidable proprietress is precarious at best and requires strict adherence to long-evolved behavior patterns that evidently prevent the female from devouring cohabitants along with the ensnared insects. I have never heard of anyone being bitten by these imposing spiders.

At the entrance to the path through the forest, a small rise (a relic dune ridge) is encountered before the path gradually descends to a low, wet area towards the middle of the woods. The live oaks in this forest are small in stature with twisting boughs that terminate in a thick, scrubby canopy, as would be expected of trees assaulted by strong sea breezes (see Glossary under *wind shearing* and *shrubbing effect*). The darkly-shaded area beneath provides an optimal environment for the shade-loving understory plants, such as devil's walking stick with its whorls of menacing thorns, sparkleberry, red bay, and beauty-berry with its spherical clusters of bright lavender berries in the fall. Wax myrtles occur here, but their scraggly appearance suggests that they prefer a sunnier environment.

Saw Palmettos

The low area toward the center of the woods is part of a system of sloughs that extend throughout the length of the South Area forest. This particular path goes through a shallower area of the slough, so this path is not as prone to flood after rains. The deeper slough habitat is not directly visible from the path, but will be visible from Riverview Drive at the end of our walk. Notice the ten-foot-tall saw palmettos on the left (west) of the path. Saw palmettos generally grow creeping along the surface of the ground with their large fan-shaped leaves standing up from their reclining stems. In my years tramping through maritime forests, I can recall only two other areas where saw palmettos grow erect like these.

The path rises as it approaches its exit onto Riverview Drive. Some openings in the wood's canopy at this end of the path have allowed young pines, cedars, yaupon holly, pepper vine, butterfly pea, and fuller-bodied wax myrtles to grow. The slough that could not be seen from the path in the middle of the woods is visible from the shoulder of the Riverview Drive about 25 yards north from the end of the path.

The Summer Waves park, across Riverview Drive, and the Waterskipark to the north were built on a landfilled section of marsh that was originally intended for a marina (see marina site harbor and landfilled area, in South Area Site map). Details on the history of the Marina Site are found on page 81.

SITE 2: South Dunes Picnic Area and Sea Circus Site

NATURAL HISTORY: Dunal forest emerging onto an ocean beach that has a history of erosion and migrating sand dunes. Sea Circus Site, a study of successive recovery of an area that was cleared and left to go *fallow* for nearly 50 years.

Since leaving Site 1, the road has drifted slightly inland, so it should not be surprising to find maritime forest on both sides of Beachview Drive at the entrance to the South Dunes Picnic Area. The oaks in the picnic area are smaller and daintier than those seen along the shell path in Site 1. Being closer to the beach, the trees are younger, the *shearline* lower, and the more youthful soil poorer. The symmetry and size of the trees being this close to the beach are surprising, and are due largely to the 20-foot-high dune ridge that traverses the back border of the park, which shields the trees from the sea breezes.

Crossing the picnic area from the parking lot, the path crosses two gully-shaped ponds. The ponds were made by digging out a preexistent slough lying between the two, now grassed-in, dune ridges. The direction of these elongated ponds reflect the northeast-southwest orientation of the dune ridges and swales characteristic of their recurved-spit origins.

DANGER
ALLIGATORS
IN POND

While climbing the stairs of the southernmost boardwalk, notice that the oaks rapidly become smaller as you ascend the leeward side of the dune ridge. At the upper level of the boardwalk, you penetrate through the *wind-sheared* canopy and see from above the shrubby crowns of the stunted trees on the seaward side of the dune ridge. Keep in mind that all these trees are approximately the same age. Figure 19 depicts the influence of the shearline on tree size in a similar condition. The saw palmettos seen here are the

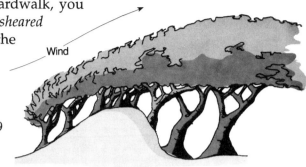

FIGURE 19: Wind Influence on Tree Growth

same as those of a forest understory. Contrary to most plants, they appear to grow equally well in the deep shade of the forest and in full sunlight, albeit, they take on the ragged, sun-bleached appearance here.

At the first turn of the descending boardwalk, the shrubby top of a large oak is seen to the right. Gazing down through the tree's thick canopy, one is astonished by the large, serpentine limbs of a well-formed live oak below. Such a tree seems out of place with the dwarfed, scrubby trees that surround it. The fact that this tree grew in a depression among sandy dunes allowed it to grow larger before reaching the shearline. Where the limbs arborize to form the canopy, they become noticeably shrubbier and backward-slanted as they come in contact with the growth-stultifying sea breezes. In my years of walking back beach areas, I never tire of being surprised by these mysterious, beautifully-sculptured, bonsaied oaks hidden among wind-shrubbed, dunal forests.

Bonsaied Oak

As we descend the boardwalk, the whole forest takes on this backward-slanting canopy similar to the forests on Beachview Drive. The resulting shearline often gives the forest the appearance of having been trimmed with hedge clippers. Aside from being wind-shorn, these stunted live oaks also tend to grow numerous smaller branches, giving them their shrubby appearance. (The glossary under *wind shearing* and *shrubbing effect* describes how the trees are shaped by the sea breezes).

Further down the boardwalk the trees and shrubs discontinue at the approach of massive sand dunes, supporting sparse communities of grasses and flowering weeds typical of those on beach meadows. The massive dunes in this area were formed with bulldozers and snow fencing, which were part of a major beach restoration project that took place in 1983. The restoration project also included the erection of the two boardwalks and the planting of native beach species.

For many years prior to the restoration project, this area was heavily trafficked by bathers going to and coming from the beach. The sand liberated from the destruction of the plant communities in the trodden areas drifted and smothered neighboring beach communities. Over decades the increasing quantities of free sand built up into large migrating dunes which smothered acres of meadow and buried trees on the seaward side of the picnic area. Such encroachments by migrating sand dunes have smothered acres of forest on Cumberland Island.

Forest encroached upon by migrating sand dunes on Cumberland Island (Notice the dead trees in the background.)

The effects of this history is seen today by comparing the beach meadow communities in the area of the boardwalk with the more-advanced shrub communities in the less-disturbed, neighboring areas in the same zone (see Figure 13, page 21, for beach zones). The present buildup and stabilization of the picnic area dunes is a testimony to the conservational effects of snow fencing and boardwalks on a beach.

At the end of the boardwalk, approximately 50 to 100 feet of sea oat-covered primary dunes and dry upper beach have formed beyond the shrubs at the time this book was written. In 1983, the *Field Guide to Jekyll Island* describes this beach as undergoing advanced erosion, with its shrubbed-covered dunes being scarped by the breakers.[21] Some of the erosion scarps are still visible. The buried steps also attest to this momentary period of *accretion*. (Steps going to a beach are often excellent measuring sticks for detecting accretion or erosion.)

The beach is broad and wet with a gradual slope, runnels, and small breakers indicating its low-energy nature. The ripples seen on both the intertidal beach and on the dry sand are created by the flow of water and wind respectively. (Our study of ripples has been reserved for the broader, accreting beach in Site 3. If you are unable to visit Site 3, the study presented there can be applied just as easily to this beach.) The closest island visible from this beach is Little Cumberland which is just north of Cumberland, the larger island seen in the distance.

After enjoying the beach, proceed north toward the entrance of the second boardwalk. This boardwalk traverses the northern extent of the disturbed area discussed above. Spectacular views of the shearline are seen as you approach the forest. This boardwalk cuts through the same large dune ridge in back of the picnic area that the other boardwalk crossed. The boardwalk leads into an opening through the wind-shrubbed, forest canopy to the shaded picnic area behind. Passing through the wooded tunnel from the shimmering sunlight to the deep shade is an enchanting experience.

Entering the picnic area, notice again the rapid rise of the tree height as the shearline ascends and the area falls behind the protective barrier of the large dune ridge. As you walk along the path skirting the back side of the dune ridge, it is difficult to believe that the trees on the top and at the bottom of the ridge are approximately the same age.

SEA CIRCUS SITE

After leaving the South Dunes Picnic Area, drive slowly south on Beachview to see the adjoining Sea Circus site. The large lot to the left, just south of the picnic area, was cleared of a maritime forest and leveled to build a Sea Circus in the 1950s, and then it was left to go *fallow*. In 40 years, this area had succeeded only to the point of supporting a beach meadow community (see Maritime Forest describing regrowth of live oak forests, page 41). In the past five or so years isolated buckthorn, wax myrtle, and red bay trees growing among the meadow plants indicate an emerging shrub forest succession. With the sea breezes, poor soil, and shifting sand, such disturbed areas recover very slowly.

Blowouts are another factor that have retarded plant succession in this area. Blowouts are the large, shallow, crater-like formations that are seen throughout this area. They are started by a disturbance, such as the soil-loosening impressions left by the feet of a running animal or people walking through an area. Sand, liberated by the disturbance, is scattered by the wind which buries and smothers surrounding plant communities and leaves an expanded cavity in the area of the original impression. The cavity continues to expand its

Large blowout with plants colonizing its center

perimeter, burying plants and liberating more sand, and it eventually becomes a crater-like blowout. Notice in the larger blowouts that the middle areas have again become colonized by plants. In these cases the middle areas have become sufficiently remote from the turbulent, wind-deflecting edges to allow colonization while the expanding edges remain bare (see illustration, page 68).

In areas of intense winds, such as the beach we just visited, we saw evidence that the sand liberated from such disturbances can build up into large, migrating dunes that can smother all vegetation in their path. Looking across the site, the high, grass-covered dune seen on the ocean side of the picnic area is a remaining part of one of the migrating dunes that was encroaching onto the park forest. Also notice the clearly-formed shearline in the wooded canopy above the picnic area. The extreme shrubbing of the trees across the road from the site has occurred as a result of the removal of the trees on the Sea Circus site that formerly shielded that area from the sea breezes, close to 50 years ago.

~

Just south of Site 2, the road is at its closest point to the beach in the South Area allowing the ocean to be visible through sea oat-covered dunes. The close proximity also accounts for the shrub forest lying on both sides of the road as you head toward the water tower. Past the water tower, the road gradually veers interiorly, so that the maritime forest again appears on the right and the shrub forest on the left, and continues this way through to St. Andrews Picnic Area. Notice that the maritime forest has a continuous *canopy* while the canopy of the shrub forest is limited to each of the individual trees. This is one of the criteria employed to differentiate between these two *ecosystems*.

SITE 3: Glory Path

NATURAL HISTORY: A transect walk through the habitat zones of an accreting ocean beach starting from a shrub forest. Water- and wind-generated ripples and related phenomena are studied, and the impact of making a movie on a beach meadow is observed.

About 1/2 mile south of the water tower is the gate which opens into a mowed field at the north end of the Jekyll Island 4-H property. Follow the automobile tracks across the field to the boardwalk. The origin for the name "Glory" for this boardwalk will be explained later.

The boardwalk starts out in a shrub forest habitat and passes over five dune ridges and swales on the way to the beach. The first swale, at the entrance of the boardwalk, is a deep slough. The presence of Carolina willows and smartweed indicate that the slough has fresh water most of the time. A rather large specimen of a Hercules' club is seen on the left side of the boardwalk, in the area of the first dune ridge. These spiny trees, sometimes referred to as prickly ash, are in the citrus family, and their leaves have the same odor and create the same astringent sensation on the lips and tongue as does the skin of an

Boardwalk over meadowed dune ridge between shrub-covered swales

orange or lemon. The numbing effect gives this plant a third name of tooth-ache tree. Some of the dune ridges within the shrub-forest community have few shrubs and support sea oats, camphorweed, and other plants associated more with primary dunes and dune meadows (see illustration at the top of the page). This apparent incongruity is explained in the Ocean Beach, page 28.

Among the sparse vegetation in the dune ridges, you may have noticed the 1 1/2- to 2-inch-diameter, perfectly-shaped, conical pits in the sand. These are made by *antlions*, named after the rapacious larval stage that dwells at the bottom of the pit awaiting prey. The walls of the pit are the steepest possible angle without having the sand tumble down. The pits are produced in seconds by underground circular movements of the antlion -- this action may be the origin of the antlion's other name, doodlebug. A small insect, usually an ant, which falls into the pit immediately attempts escape by scrambling up the pit wall, setting off an avalanche of sand carrying the victim to the ice-pick-like jaws poised at the bottom. If the victim is able to

Antlion Pits

successfully climb against the cascading sand, the antlion flicks sand in its direction, further loosening the sand under the scurrying prey.

One can induce the sand-flicking behavior of the antlion by carefully dropping sand, a few grains at a time, on the sloping pit wall, simulating a crawling ant. To capture one of these 1/4- to 1/2-inch doodlebugs, scoop up the pit with some of the surrounding sand into the cup of your hands and allow the sand to trickle out the small openings between your fingers, leaving the harmless bug in your hand. (More is said about the identification and curious life history of the *antlion* in the Glossary.)

Antlion

With the passage of each dune ridge, the hybrid oaks, buckthorn, and other shrub-forest trees in the swales become smaller in stature, and wax myrtles increase in number. About 2/3 of the way along the boardwalk, you enter the shrub zone. The shrub composition becomes mostly wax myrtles with a scattering of groundsel trees. The shrub zone is quite narrow and its well-defined seaward edge, where it meets the beach meadow, is quickly reached.

Typical of an accreting beach, the beach-meadow is fairly extensive. Besides having the representative dune-meadow plants (Appendix A), partridge-pea, a roadside weed, colors the older, back-meadows with its rich, gold, red-centered flowers in the fall. The appearance of isolated clumps of young wax myrtle in the middle of the beach-meadow zone indicate areas of shrub-zone *succession*.

Partridge Pea

About 500 feet to the south of the boardwalk, an almost pure stand of partridge-pea, spangled with wax myrtle, extends from the shrub zone well into the primary dunes, covering more than an acre (at the time of this writing). This is the site where the film-ing of the movie, *Glory*, took place about five years ago (see South Area Site map, Figure 17). After the filming, artificial dunes were shaped, sprigged with dune grasses, and regularly watered until the grasses became established. Evidently this impact greatly stepped up succession of this area causing plants characteristic of older meadows and clusters of wax myrtles to grow throughout the entire meadow. A short walk down the beach is worth-while to see what subsequent successional changes may have occurred. Besides an excellent movie production, a benefit that remains from the movie is the boardwalk that we have been using, which was constructed to transport actors and props to the movie set.

Before descending the stairs to the beach, notice that the dune meadows of the beaches to the north are narrower than those to the south. This is in keeping with recurved spits whose beaches increase in size as one goes south (see Geology, page 17). The broad, flat face of this beach with its runnels and abundant dune meadows, offers an excellent opportunity to study and compare water- and wind-produced *ripples*.

RIPPLE STUDY

Ripples left in the exposed wet beach are formed by water movement over the sand surface or by wavelets in standing or slowly-moving water.

The size and shape of water-flow ripples are a function of the speed of the water movement. A moderate flow creates sinuous ripples, seen in the illustration of ripple patterns on the next page. An increase in flow rate will produce larger and more widely-spaced sinuous ripples as long as the flow remains *laminar*. Further increase in flow speed eventually produces *turbulence* which induces irregular, angular movements of the water. The turbulent movement cuts angular grooves or *rills* through the uniform sinuous ripples creating linguoid (tongue-shaped) ripples which appear more like laid tile. When wa-ter rushes at high speeds, it shears off the surface of the sand leaving it flat and featureless. The fast-moving water in the inlet channel of the North End Beach offers excellent conditions for the observation of shearing and the curious phenomenon of *antidune* formation, which we shall describe in Site 8.

Sinuous Ripples

Linguoid Ripples

Ripples produced by wavelets are also sinuous and may appear at first like those produced by flowing water, but closer examination of their cross sections reveals their symmetrical shapes and sharp-edged crests. These are especially uncomfortable to walk over in bare feet. Water-flow ripples, on the other hand, are asymmetrical in cross section with their steeper faces on the down-current sides of the ripple (see ripple cross-section diagram below). Various combinations of these two types of ripples are often found in hard-packed intertidal sand. The Glossary under *ripples* describes the mechanics of the formation of both water-flow and wave-produced ripples. Consultation of this section of the Glossary would be helpful in the understanding of ripple form and behavior, especially in light of the coming paragraphs.

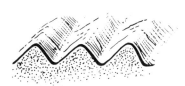

Symmetrical Ripples

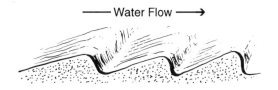

— Water Flow ⟶

Asymmetrical Ripples

If the water is moving, especially in a *runnel,* you may be able to watch ripples form and migrate in the water flow. Close observation may allow you to see the sand grains and darker mineral sediments moving along the sand surface with the flowing water. Because of the different density, shape and size of their particles, the minerals and the whiter sand tend to deposit (*sort out*) onto different areas along the ripple faces (see Glossary under *sorting out of sediments*). Such a process produces horizontal, subsurface banding patterns called *cross bedding* as layers of sand accumulate over time (see illustration on opposing page). (More is said about structure and significance of *cross bedding* in the Glossary.) If the water is too cloudy to see the sand movement or the tide is not right, there may be an opportunity to see better the particle movement and sorting in the dry sand under the influence of the wind.

The broad beach meadow and upper-beach development present ideal conditions to study how dry sand responds to wind. A moderate wind flow sufficient to move sand grains usually leaves sinuous ripples similar to those created by water. Unlike water-generated ripples, a faster flow does not produce the higher-energy linguoid ripples. Instead, the sinuous ripples continue to grow larger and further apart. These continue to grow until the wind velocity reaches a critical speed which, similar to the fast moving water, planes the sand surface flat. At this point, *sand dunes* may form where shells, tidal wrack or other objects interrupt the air flow over the surface of the sand (see Glossary for the process of *sand dune* formation).

If the wind is sufficient to move sand grains, you can watch the sand and the darker mineral materials bouncing and creeping over the ripple surface. As in flowing water, the darker, denser minerals do not move as far nor as fast as the sand and therefore tend to be deposited at the base of the ripples. The lighter, whiter sand tends to settle on the crests and the leeward slopes of the ripples. Even if the wind is not blowing, the distribution of the sand and minerals along the ripple surfaces is still visible. If there is a blustery wind on the beach, you can watch the blown sand form a dune within seconds by using your foot or any other object to interrupt the wind flow on the beach surface.

Similar to the wet sand, the sorted sediments form into *cross beds*, but they are not as observable, because the sand falls apart with attempts to expose them (see Glossary on *cross bedding*). However, with a high-velocity wind, layer after layer of sand is planed off the surface revealing the cross bedding as intricate, wood-grain-like patterns as seen in the illustration at the bottom right. The variously layered and angled cross beds become like contour lines in a topographical map. You can watch these patterns change as the wind strips off the surface layers and the underlying, differently-oriented cross beds become exposed. These constantly-changing, sand-blasted patterns are one of nature's most dynamic art displays.

Vertically cut-away section of
beach showing cross bedding

Cross bedding exposed on the
surface of wind-stripped sand

Chameleon

On the way back to the vehicles, anoles (small green or brown lizards) are often encountered scurrying along the boardwalk during the warmer months. The green anole (*Anolis carolinensis*) is the only native representative of a family of tropical eguanid lizards. Anoles are commonly, but erroneously, referred to as chameleons because of their ability to change their usual green color to brown or gray to blend with the background. As you can see from the drawings, the appearances of chameleons and anoles are markedly different as are their geographic locations -- chameleons are exclusively *Old World* while most of the anoles are *New World*. Chameleons are the true masters of disguise, being able to conceal themselves by adopting background patterns with multiple colors. You may have an opportunity to see the anoles flex their red throat fans and bob their heads as they engage in courtship or territorial displays.

Anole

~

The Jekyll Island 4-H center is visible to the south from the field at the foot of the Glory boardwalk, and is passed on Beachview Drive going south towards St. Andrews Picnic Area (see South Area Site map). The center offers a variety of environmental education programs for school groups throughout Georgia and neighboring states. In the summer it offers training programs for teachers and it is a camp for 4-H members. The facility, with its dormitory, dining hall and teaching areas, has a capacity for 150 participants. The center houses and instructs more than 20,000 people a year. This author conceived the environmental program and coordinated the founding of the facility with the University of Georgia Cooperative Extension Service in 1983.

A small development of homes is seen just west of the 4-H Center. The seaward-most homes were constructed on beachfront property in the early 1970s. With the accretion of the south-end beach over the years, the houses now overlook a 1/4 mile of low shrub and meadows, interspersed with wetlands (see Homes on the South Area Site map). We shall again see this accreted area from St. Andrews Sound Beach, Site 5.

Just opposite the entrance to St. Andrews, where the bike path crosses Beachview Drive, there is a forested dune ridge whose road-side slope is fairly clear of underbrush and is an easy climb. From the top of the ridge there is a spectacular view of the forest floor covered with saw palmettos. The relic dune ridges at this more southern location are considerably larger than the ones seen along the shell path in Site 1. This part of the island is younger, and the dune ridges and swales are much more pronounced.

SITE 4: St. Andrews Sound and Picnic Area

NATURAL HISTORY: A narrow, forested upland with high-relief dune ridges and swales. Many of the dune ridges traverse the marsh east of the upland. The beach of St. Andrews Sound forms the western border of the upland.

The hilly nature of this southwestern location is immediately noticeable upon entering the picnic area. The park is in a forest dominated by pines and sand live oaks (*Quercus geminata*) and has a zone of red cedars close to the beach. Sand live oaks are squat and often have two or more main trunks arising from the ground; hence, the name, *geminata*, meaning twin. Close examination of one of the large slash pines in the parking area reveals a loosely-layered, plated bark. The fire-resistant capability of the bark of this and other species of southern yellow pine is detailed in the Maritime Forest section, page 41.

Our walk begins following the well-trodden path leading up the large, forested dune ridge across the drive from the parking lot. At the foot of the dune ridge is a large, heavily-trunked live oak, festooned with *epiphytes* (illustrated). Among these are two *bromeliads*, Spanish moss (*Tillandsia usneoides*), and the rarer ball moss

The large oak at the foot of the dune ridge

(*T. recurvata*). Being bromeliads, neither of these are mosses, but flowering plants. A true moss, for comparison, is the dark-green mat of soft, tiny plantlets seen on shaded sides of the tree's large boughs and trunk. Both bromeliads are covered with silvery scales, called trycomes, which absorb water and nutrients from the air. Spanish moss has a modest, green, three-petaled flower at the ends of its branching filaments which appears for two to three weeks in May. Its thin brown seed pods remain attached and can be seen any time of year (See illustration on top of page 76). The flowers and seed-heads of the ball moss are on stalks and are readily visible throughout the year. Clumps of the coarser ball moss can be found attached to rotting stems which have fallen to the ground. This tree is one of a few locations where the more tropical ball moss is found on the Georgia coast. Ball moss gets its name from its ball-like clusters around utility wires, a common sight in the wire-shrouded streets of the Caribbean Islands.

Ball moss

Resurrection Fern

Lichen

flower

Spanish Moss

pod

A common misconception that Spanish moss is a parasite to trees is largely supported by a tendency for the plants to be concentrated on dead limbs. Dead limbs simply offer better access to sunlight without the competition of leaves. The gray of the Spanish moss blends with the dark green of the oak leaves giving the coastal forests their unique gray-green color. Spanish moss also lends a slight pungent odor to the forest, especially after a rain.

Resurrection fern is another *epiphyte* growing on live oaks. It gets its name from the way its brown, curled leaves "resurrect" by uncurling and turning green for several days after rain. Since tree bark does not hold water well and rains are often erratic, going into a dormant state during dry periods conserves the fern's energy and reduces death due to dehydration. This epiphytic fern draws its nutrients from the decaying bark and airborne materials and water that get trapped in the fern's furry fronds.

Among this veritable vegetable garden of epiphytes on these great oaks are a variety of lichens. A lichen is a *commensalistic* relationship between a fungus and blue-green algae. The fungus provides a protective housing, water and nutrients for itself and the algae living within its cells. The algae supplies food, through photosynthesis, for both organisms. Lichens come in a variety of shapes indicative of their species. Most lichens are blue-green colored, due to the algae's chlorophyll. A curious red-colored lichen gets its color by the periodic production of red fruiting bodies by the host fungus, *Haematomma elatunum*. The genus name is adopted from the medical term, hematoma, referring to the reddish discolorations caused by bleeding under the skin. Locals sometimes call it bubble gum lichen. Before leaving the great oak, notice the many, shade-loving, elephant's foot plants on the ground under its spreading limbs. Their rosettes of furry leaves carpet the ground and on stalks are clusters of small lavender flowers.

Elephant's foot

Follow the path to the top of the dune ridge, down through the swale, and up over the second ridge. Notice that the tidal wash from the marsh to the right extends into the swale we crossed. From the top of the second dune ridge, continue down a gradual decline to a little sandy beach to the right of the path which overlooks the marsh.

Standing on the marsh beach, see the forested dune ridge across the narrow section of high marsh in front of you. This long, thin dune ridge (dune ridge #1 in the North Area Site map) traverses the marsh to the east. Looking at the Site map, only a few, relic dune ridges traverse the marsh. More than likely, there were many more of these dune ridges at an earlier time, but meandering tidal creeks have eroded them away over the years by a process similar to that shown in Figure 16, page 36. A meander which has cut through dune ridge #1 can be seen a short distance along its length -- a continuation of dune reduction in progress.

The tall grass growing along the edge of this little beach is bunch grass (*Spartina bakeri*), a freshwater species. Bunch grass appears similar to its salt-marsh cousin, salt meadow cordgrass (*S. patens*), but it is taller and colonizes into dense circular bunches, hence its name. Bunch grass grows here because of the freshwater runoff from the surrounding woodlands. This same runoff is why the glasswort and saltwort are so robust and tall in this patch of high marsh.

To get to dune ridge #1, you may walk across the narrow section of high marsh, or backtrack to the edge of the woods and follow the path that skirts around the marsh edge. The path dead ends into the path that runs along the length of dune ridge #1. Turn right and follow the path which very shortly ends where the meandering creek, mentioned earlier, completely cuts through the dune ridge. Notice that the same tidal creek is currently eroding the north side of the ridge leaving its telltale scarp.

Coming back from the cut, the path along the dune ridge leads to the northern end of the picnic area. On the way, notice that the creek meanders between this dune ridge and the one on the other side, north of the narrow marsh (dune ridge #2 on the Site map). Notice with each turn of the creek, mud is deposited on the inside of the turns, forming point bars, and eroded on the outside consistent with what one would expect of a meander (see Glossary on *meandering*). Approaching the picnic area, you stand on a steep bluff where large trees have been undercut and have fallen. Notice that the creek below has taken a sharp horseshoe turn creating these severe erosion conditions on our bank, the outside swing of the turn.

Erosion Scarps

Point Bar

FIGURE 23: Direction of Water Movement in a Meandering Creek

As we enter the north end of the picnic area, we can see that the tidal creek which we have been following continues to the beach where it opens to the sound a short distance away. A larger creek which irrigates the marsh on the other side (north) of dune ridge #2 merges with our creek to form the *inlet*. The beach of St. Andrews Sound also ends at this inlet. From this point, you may follow the path along the edge of the woods or walk the sound beach back to the parking area before venturing onto the beach phase of this walk, Site 5.

SITE 5: St. Andrews Sound Beach

NATURAL HISTORY: A sound beach leading to the southernmost and young-est point on Jekyll Island. The eroding sound shore transects all of the zones of the accreting ocean beach which it eventually adjoins.

From the beach in front of the little boardwalk, the view is due west across the upper reaches of St. Andrews Sound. The land-forms across the sound are marsh and marsh hammocks divided by the five rivers that converge into St. Andrews Sound. In the distance is the mainland area of Dover Bluff.

The St. Andrews Sound Beach is intertidal and is covered with water for about an hour during the maximum height of the tide. A look at the tide table before walking the beach is advised. The sound beach joins the ocean beach about 1/2 mile to the south. That intersection of the two beaches is the south-ernmost point and youngest part of Jekyll Island.

The South Area Site map shows that the sound beach cuts across the rows of dune ridges forming this southern extreme of the island. The undulating land profile seen throughout the duration of your walk on the sound beach is the transected view of the dune ridges and swales coming toward the beach. (This transected view may be visualized by the ripple cross-section diagram in the middle of page 72.) Erosion scarps and fallen trees indicate the history of erosion. The beach has a steep drop-off with a fast current running close to the beach. Wakes from boats moving along this shoreline greatly exacerbate ero-sion during the higher tides when the water washes the upper beach and dunes.

These conditions do, however, favor seining for shrimp which often move close to the shore with the fast-moving waters. Seiners working this beach never seem to mind curious visitors looking over their catch as long as they are not interrupted too much. You can see from what was caught in the seine, that the fish and invertebrates which move in the marshes and sounds are highly diverse but small in size (see list on the opposite page). Shrimp, blue crabs, and mullet are the principal animals sought by the seiners, and occasionally, a larger flounder, whiting or sea trout is taken with the catch.

Seiners fishing on the beach

```
List of fish and invertebrates commonly caught in seines:

Fish:                              Invertebrates:

flounder, hogchoker, mullet,       blue crab, mud crab, lady crab,
spot, croaker, star drum,          hermit crab, spider crab,
whiting, sea catfish,              leopard crab, grass shrimp,
mummichog, killifish,              commercial shrimp, mantis shrimp,
silversides, anchovy,              sea pansy, sea whip, jellyfish,
menhaden (pogy), blenny,           jellyball, hairy cucumber, starfish,
sea trout, filefish, pipefish,     brittle star, mud star, sand dollar,
sea robin, Atlantic bumper,        marsh snail, oyster drill,
pompano, lookdown, yellowtail      whelk, moon snail, squid
```

At the onset of our walk, the live oak-pine-cedar maritime forest quickly transforms into a buckthorn-shrub forest. Close to this point of transition lies a wetland which occasionally receives a tidal flow when a temporary inlet opens up through the beach. Proceeding further down the beach, the trees and bushes of the shrub forest become smaller with an increase of cedars and wax myrtles. The approach of the shrub zone is determined by the predominance of wax myrtles with scattered groundsel trees. The front edge of the shrub zone where it meets with the grassy meadows is again clearly defined.

The meadow is complicated by two small, inconsistent inlets which, when flowing, bring tidal waters into the meadow. A full spectrum of wetland plants ranging from salt to freshwater occupy this large preserve. Their distribution throughout the area reflects the degree of tidal inundation to the various areas of the wetland. Sea oxeye daisy, salt meadow cordgrass and nut grasses occupy much of the wetland close to the sound beach, and fiddler villages line the banks of the capricious, little tidal channels. Most of the dune ridges in the meadow are in the form of small hammocks, some presently supporting dune meadow plants and others wax myrtles.

The homes appearing about 1/4 mile behind the sloughs and hammocks are the ones we passed shortly before arriving at St. Andrews Picnic Area (see Homes in the South Area Site map, Figure 17). It is difficult to believe that the houses actually fronted the ocean beach in the early 1970s, when the neighborhood was developed. This entire meadow and developing shrub zone at the time of this writing is only 25 years old.

At the approach to the southern point of the island, well-formed primary dunes topped with sea oats and beach elder are encountered. Even though the primary dunes are growing along the ocean beach, the dunes that extend

Brown Pelican
fishing offshore

79

to the sound beach are perpendicularly scarped by erosion. Where the scarps cut into dunes supporting sea oats, one can often see previous generations of buried sea oats connected together by vertical runners with the surface plants. In these almost perfect, cross-sectional views, the buried plant bodies of the sea oats are recognized by the clusters of roots and fragments of dead leaves along the verticle runners. (See sea oat illustration and an interpretation of nature's competitive strategy for this pattern of growth on the bottom of page 27.)

Black Skimmer fishing inshore

Massive shoals occur at the point where the ocean and sound currents meet. The ocean beach here is the growing end of Jekyll's recurved spit. Accordingly, ocean beaches in such a vicinity tend to build rapidly. The rapid growth of this beach is evidenced by the extensive system of meadows and sloughs we passed and which are visible behind the primary dunes. The continued growth of the island is seen in the incipient dunes (sometimes several in number) in front of the primary dunes on the ocean beach. Many of these are only weeks old. Barring any distructive storms, these incipient dunes may soon become primary dunes. Most of the primary dunes were formed this year. The older primary dunes are left behind as dune ridges as the beach grows eastward. Thus, the island grows dune ridge by dune ridge, like the growth rings of a tree.

With the thousands of shorebirds that gather on these shoals and beaches, and the nesting that takes place in the beach meadows and sloughs, this area is the most important bird sanctuary on the island. Birding is excellent here. About a half mile up the ocean beach is the Jekyll Island 4-H Center, so it is not unusual to encounter student groups exploring this area and St. Andrews beach. The islands of Cumberland and Little Cumberland are seen to the south. Return to the picnic area for the next phase of our field trip which takes us north on Riverview Drive.

Gulls, terns and skimmers gathered on shoals

Most of Riverview skirts between the western edge of the maritime forest and the salt marsh. Several dune ridges coming from the maritime forest and going across the marsh are seen from Riverview Drive. The first of these is seen to the right of the road, a short distance west of the entrance to St. Andrews Picnic Area. Although the dune ridges are not well defined, the swale lying between them is visible. This particular swale supports a needle rush marsh.

Over the next 3/4 mile, you pass two roads to the right which lead into the maritime forest. A short distance (1/10 mile) past the second road, you come to a second marshy slough bordered by dune ridges on the right. Pull over to the left side of the road close to a concrete culvert identified by a small, white survey marker. The slough to the right of the road is supplied with water from the marsh which runs under the road through the culvert. The oak-covered dune ridge on the southern border of the slough continues on the left side of the road as it runs across the marsh to the southwest. The illustration depicts the dune ridge as seen from the culvert. The South Area Site map locates both the dune ridge (labeled #3) and the culvert.

Dune ridge crossing marsh

Dune ridge fragment

View of marsh from the culvert

A fragment of another dune ridge, in the form of a large, live-oak hammock, is seen in the marsh just opposite the culvert (see illustration). The origin of this dune ridge has been obliterated by the landfill to the north. The rambling mixture of cedars, young pines, groundsel trees, wax myrtles, saltcedars, and dog fennel to the northwest demarcate the southern extent of the landfill for the marina site, mentioned in Site 1.

About 1/10 mile north of the culvert, stop at the chain-linked entrance gate to the marina site. If the site is still closed to the public, it is visible through the chain-link fence. In 1968 a 36-acre yacht harbor, and freshwater pond were dredged in the marsh and the spoils were used as land fill surrounding the harbor. The freshwater pond was employed to float yachts to *osmotically* kill barnacles and other saltwater fouling organisms attached to their bottoms, so that the organisms were easier to scrape off. The marina project was abandoned because the harbor filled in with mud shortly after it was dredged and saltwater seeped into the pond. Today the fill area houses the two water parks to the north, Summer Waves and Waterskipark. Waterskipark currently uses the pond for a cable-driven water-ski tow. The harbor, at this point, continues to remain idle, filled with mud, and with the recent invasion of cordgrass, it appears to be succeeding back to a salt marsh.

Across Riverview Drive from the marina site is a needle-rush marsh bordered by dune ridges. Any evidence of the continuation of the dune ridges through the marsh on the west side of the road has been obliterated by the landfill. The oak hammock that we saw from the culvert may have been a fragment of the more southern of these dune ridges.

Approaching the Ben Fortson Parkway, the ponds and watery sloughs coursing through the maritime forest to the right are of a character and pattern different from those seen through the rest of the South End. This is believed to be the southern-most extent of the system of uplands and sloughs formed from the recurved spits of the Holocene island that fronted Jekyll Island before the formation of the South Area below this point. Views of this ancient system of sloughs and uplands are also seen from Ben Fortson Parkway and from Riverview Drive approaching the Jekyll Island Club grounds in Site 6.

SITE 6: Mid-island Sloughs

NATURAL HISTORY: The Pleistocene-Holocene border of Jekyll Island, tidal marshes and sloughs, and the impact of an early attempt to control tidal circulation through those marshes.

Going north on Riverview from Ben Fortson Parkway, the road passes over the northern section of the intricate slough system seen from the Ben Fortson Parkway and areas immediately south. The northern extent of this system is bordered by Stable and Shell Roads. As mentioned at the end of the previous section, this mid-island, wetland system is believed to be a remnant of the re-curved spit formation of the Holocene island that at one time fronted the entire Island before most of South Area was formed.

Concrete storm drains connected by a culvert are seen on both sides of the road just before the entrance sign to the Jekyll Island Club, at the fork of Riverview and Stable Roads. This and a smaller inlet that was crossed on the way are the only avenues for tide waters to enter and leave this entire mid-island marsh system. The Ben Fortson Parkway blocks any tidal communication of this marsh system with its ramifications to the south. The abundance of needle rush, randomly-situated shrub hammocks, and large bodies of stagnant, algae-choked waters are signs of this system's poor tidal circulation.

Turn right onto Stable Road and slow down where there is a clear view of the marsh to the right. At the opposite end of this marsh, where it narrows down to a creek entrance, there are the remains of a tidal gate that was constructed by the Jekyll Island Club to control tidal flow to a large, interior section of this marsh, called the Duck Pond (see South Area map, Figure 17). The creek entrance is behind a bank of trees so the gate is not visible from here. The creek connecting the tidal gate to the Duck Pond was straightened and diked to prevent other tidal influences from entering the pond system. Anticipating the most favorable periods for duck hunting, the tidal gate was closed to block both the inflow of the tide and the outflow of freshwater from rains. Enough freshwater was supposed to be trapped to create a sizable pond to attract wild ducks and other water fowl. For all the damage this project brought to the mid-island marshes, historical sources say that the Duck Pond did not work very well.[22]

Near the corner of Shell and Stable Roads is the northern entrance to the bike path leading to the Pleistocene-Holocene border of Jekyll and to the Duck Pond. Those in automobiles may turn off the road to the right, park at the edge of the woods near the bike path, and walk. The path descends for a little over 2/10 mile through a pine-oak forest to the wetlands below. The path levels off and skirts eastward along the edge of the wetland. Much of the path delineates, in the opinion of the author, the approximate border between the Pleistocene uplands to the north and the intermittent wetlands of the Holocene, recurved-spit system to the south.

Diamond-back Terrapin

Follow the path to the bridge overlooking the Duck Pond. Notice the diked sides of the tidal creek and salt-to-brackish wetlands that surround its banks. In spite of the diking of this major creek, some of the surrounding marshlands remained sufficiently inundated by tidal waters from the other sources to allow the Jekyll Island Club to keep terrapins in "turtle pens." Some of the stakes supporting the pens are still standing. Diamond-backed terrapin stew was a great delicacy in those days.

This part of the bike path is an old road which likewise was built upon a dike. A short way along the path a half-acre pond is encountered. The inordinate depth of the pond and the fact that it has no outlet suggests that it was a "borrow-pit" from which fill material was taken to build the dikes. The pond is evidently fed by the rains and has a full complement of floating and emergent freshwater plants. Look for a large alligator that frequents this pond, but do not disturb nor attempt to feed it. (It will not disturb you, if you do not disturb it.)

83

The bike path bridges over the creek close to its junction with the Duck Pond marsh to the east. The high flow speed of the tide waters through this narrow area comes as no surprise with the realization that this is the only avenue through which this enormous marsh is tidally irrigated. The oysters attached to the tabby bridge ruins below reap an abundance of suspended food from the rushing waters. The presence of needle rush throughout the marsh is an indication of low salinity due to a combination of poor tidal circulation and freshwater runoff from the surrounding uplands.

A look at either of the Jekyll Island maps, Figures 4 or 17, shows the close juxtaposition of the northern part of the Duck Pond with the golf course pond on the other side of Shell Road. From this appearance, one might presume that they are part of the same watershed, but the two areas do not communicate. An 1889 United States Coastal Survey map of Jekyll shows that no ponds existed between Captain Wylly and Shell Roads.[23] The ponds in that area were more than likely formed from borrow pits to supply fill materials for the construction of the golf course.[22]

For those on foot, there is really little else of significance to see beyond the bridge, so the shortest route would be for you to return to your vehicles the way you came. The bicycles could continue to follow the path to the Ben Fortson Parkway and go north on Riverview Road to continue the tour. After returning to your vehicles, a visit to the museum, just ahead on Stable Road, and to the Jekyll Island Club grounds recreates the grandeur of the turn-of-the-century life that took place on Jekyll -- a worthwhile experience.

*Faith Chapel,
Jekyll Island Club*

NORTH AREA

The North Area extends from Shell Road to the North End Beach. Most of the northern area of Jekyll has been greatly modified by people over the years. A review of the history section describes clearing and tilling of these rich Pleistocene soils for Sea Island Cotton during the Plantation Period. Later much of this same land was developed and modified for the various uses of the Jekyll Island Club. Today home sites, golf courses, a shopping center and waste landfill occupy much of this area. The focus of this section of the guide, then, is directed to areas along the shoreline where natural land features and residing ecological communities can be found.

Continuing North On Riverview Drive

After visiting the Jekyll Island Club, continue north on Stable Road and onto Riverview Drive. A young but mature, oak-pine maritime forest that covers most of the North Area of the island has been growing since the plantation days, which date many of the older trees to be between 100 to 130 years old. Because of a common history of vigorous cultivation of the Golden Isles during the plantation era, many of the mature trees on St. Simons and Sapelo Islands are the same age.[6]

The road passes by houses and churches on the right. The views of the marsh through the silhouettes of curvaceous oaks, especially during sunset, are a daily blessing for the people living in those homes. Riding the bike paths that weave in and out of the trees bordering the marsh is an especially rewarding way to visit this area of the island.

On the way to the north end of the island is the ruin of Major Horton's house (see History, page 49). The house, like so many early constructions, was made of tabby. *Tabby* is an ingenious answer to construction needs in the early days in the absence of stone and concrete (see Glossary). The red bay growing at the northwest corner of the Horton house is an exceptionally large specimen.

On the other side of Beachview Drive is the duBignon Burial Ground. The picnic area surrounding the burial ground retains the impression of its bucolic past with the cedars, oaks and pines scattered in a ground cover of broomsedges, bristlegrass, and switch grass, so typical of fallow farm fields. The two active tidal creeks that closely skirt the picnic grounds offer an opportunity to observe the plant and animal communities of the creek banks and plant zonation of the marsh leading to the upland area of the picnic grounds.

SITE 7: Clam Creek Picnic Area and Fishing Pier

NATURAL HISTORY: Meandering marsh creek eroding an upland, view of the western shore of Jekyll's Holocene formation, and an analysis of oyster colony formation on pilings.

The entrance to Clam Creek Road is approximately 1/2 mile north of the duBignon Burial Ground. Clam Creek Road lies on a thin remnant of Pleistocene upland which, over the years, has been eroded to this attenuated state by the meandering Clam Creek. After passing through a short stretch of young mixed forest, the first of the three meanders currently attacking this strip of land appears.   Compare this particular horseshoe-shaped meander with the one in Figure 24 in Glossary, under *meandering*.   Events similar to those diagrammed in the illustration may in time take place here, causing the eroding loop to turn into an oxbow, which would temporarily alleviate the erosion in this area of the roadbed. Notice the two oxbows formed by Clam Creek pointed out in the North Area Site map, page 61.

As you pass by the other two meanders on the way to the fishing pier, it is not hard to imagine that this narrow strip of land eventually could be cut into segments similar to those diagrammed in Figure 16, page 36. The armoring of the creek banks with poured concrete and rubble is an attempt to prevent this from happening. For the time, these meandering erosion sites are favorite areas for fishing and crabbing as the drawing below depicts. These erosion sites allow easy access to a deep tidal creek close to the road, which offers an excellent opportunity to sample or collect tidal creek water and aquatic life.

The upland on the other side of Clam Creek marsh is the backside of Jekyll's remaining Holocene island fragment (see North Area Site map). At one time the entire Pleistocene island of Jekyll was fronted by the Holocene island which then extended from its present fragment to the area of the Ben Fortson Parkway. At that time, all of Jekyll's Pleistocene beach was a marsh shoreline with a view similar to what we are seeing (see drawing below).

FISHING PIER

The Fishing pier provides an almost 300-degree view overlooking St. Simons Sound and the North End Beach on the other side of Clam Creek marsh. Across the sound are the southern end of St. Simons Island and the arching bridges of the F. J. Torras Causeway to St. Simons. Brunswick is on the mainland far to the west. The smokestacks belong to the pulp and paper mill of Georgia Pacific and the chemical plant, Hercules.

The large, box-shaped ships moving across the sound carry foreign cars to Colonel's Island for finishing and distribution. The carriers come surprisingly close to the fishing pier as they follow the ship channel to the Brunswick River. Due to the proximity of the fishing pier to the ship channel, the waters under the pier run deep and swiftly. Unfortunately, the fish that would normally be attracted to the shelter of the pilings are carried away with fast-moving currents. Concrete rubble and discarded foundations have been placed in the waters behind the pier in an attempt to slow the water movement and to improve fishing.

On a lower tide, a ball-shaped cluster of oysters can be seen attached to each of the pier pilings. The location and shape of these clusters are a result of the interaction of biological and physical influences on the lives of the oysters. Within limits, oysters are able to live in the *intertidal* zone since they are able to close their valves (shells)

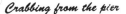
Crabbing from the pier

sealing in water during periods of air exposure; but they do require a certain, minimal amount of time under water to breath, filter-feed, and carry out other biological functions. Oysters would occupy the more optimal, *subtidal* zones but those that do are grazed away by rapacious oyster drills (see illustration on the following page). Since oyster drills have little tolerance for air exposure, the intertidal oysters survive. (In areas, such as Appalachicola, Florida, where salinity of the water is

Oysters on piling

lower than can be tolerated by the drills, subtidal oysters abound making these areas the nation's top oyster producers.) The life of the Atlantic-coast oyster, then, is a compromise that squeezes the oyster's living environment between a predator on one end and a critical time of air exposure on the other.

Oyster Drills

The large, jay-sized, black birds that dominate the park area are boat-tailed grackles. Their raucous calls and willingness to share people's lunches attract much attention. The males are shiny black with feathers that *refract* light, producing a purple-blue iridescence when exposed to the sunlight. The smaller females, with their soft brown, non-reflecting feathers, are often mistakenly regarded as another species. The long, keel-shaped tail of the male gives this southern, coastal grackle its name.

Boat-tailed grackle (male)

SITE 8: Clam Creek Bridge and North End Beach

NATURAL HISTORY: A comparison of inlets to two marshes, one well irrigated and the other periodically penetrated by the tides; an eroding sound beach; and observations of wave refraction and behaviors of the deltas, meanders, and antidunes.

Take the path leading to the bridge over Clam Creek. The bridge connects Jekyll's Pleistocene formation to the Holocene island fragment to the east. As you stand on the bridge facing the marsh, consider that approximately 35 thousand years ago the ocean washed the western shore of Clam Creek marsh, and the land to the east did not exist. With the formation of the Holocene island fronting Jekyll, the shoreline to the east appeared and the area between the land masses filled in to form the marsh. Over the years the Holocene island was reduced by erosion to its present fragment whose southern end extends from an area just north of the North Beach Picnic Area, where its ocean inlet was located (see inlet site #1 in the North Area Site map, page 61). Eventually the longshore currents deposited sand across the ocean inlet leaving Clam Creek with only one inlet, over which you are standing. Since this is the only tidal opening to the entire marsh, the flow through the inlet is rapid. Fish, crab and shrimp ride these currents as daily commuters between the sound and the marsh. The fishing lures dangling on the utility wire are evidence of people's pursuit of commuters.

From the east end of the bridge, examples of wave *refraction* can be observed as waves often curl around the curved edge of the Holocene beach. To see just how much the waves nearest you may have refracted, note the direction of their movement, and compare it to the direction of the waves moving further offshore.

Critical depth for the breaking of waves is also seen from the bridge. As waves move toward the shallow shore of the west end of the bridge, the intervals between waves become shorter and the waves begin to break, while the same waves moving over the deeper inlet channel do not exhibit these changes. (See *breakers* in Glossary for an explanation of critical depth and the mechanics of wave breaking.)

NORTH END BEACH

The length of the beach to its northeasternmost extremity is about 1/3 mile. The beach can be walked throughout most of the tidal cycle except at maximum high tide, and if the tide becomes too high while taking this walk, there is an alternative, upland path in the woods which leads back to the bridge. The name "boneyard beach" aptly describes both this and the North Beach, Site 9, because of the many trees laid over and partly buried in the intertidal sands.

Since the dredging of the ship channel at the turn of the century, the erosion of most of Jekyll's North Area beaches has been severe. This beach has retreated more than a thousand feet. The ship channel swallows up most of the sand drifting southward in the longshore currents from Sea Island and the other islands to the north. The sand that would normally be nourishing Jekyll's beaches is dredged out of the channel annually. The ship channel has also been identified as a cause for the erosion of most of St. Simons' beaches.[24]

As you walk the beach, observe the areas where the forest has been undercut by erosion. Notice the heavy thatch-work of entangled roots and saw palmetto stems that are exposed. It is through this dense underlying fabric that the trees and understory plants of a live oak maritime forest work together to resist being blown over. The recently fallen live oaks best show their shallow, spreading root system. Without the support of the forest, isolated live oaks are susceptible to falling during storms, as is so frequently the case in Georgia's coastal cities and suburbs. Also notice, on the dead oaks that have lost their bark, how the grain spirals. This contributes to the great strength of live oaks in nature and as lumber used in the live oak war ships of the early nineteenth century (see H i s t o r y, page 50).

89

Although few pine trees are found lying on this beach, their root systems are commonly seen in the sand. Unlike oaks, pines have deep, vertical roots with less spread. When a pine finally falls, it snaps at the roots, leaving the roots in the sand while the tree is carried off during a storm. The illustration shows the typical radiating pattern which identify the pine roots emerging from the sand. Excellent examples of pines in varying stages of exposure and falling are seen in Site 9, so more will be said about pine root structure there. The identification of the dense rootlet stubble occasionally seen in the sand is revealed with the denuded saw palmetto branches at the eroded edges of the forest.

Pine Roots

Close to the northeast point of the island, a second marsh appears -- the one which separates the easternmost beach from the rest of the Holocene formation (see North Area Site map). The shoreline on the western side of the marsh was the oceanfront until the land to the east formed (most likely) from a large shoal which stabilized to become an island. Similar to Clam Creek, a marsh formed between the land masses. This is a good example of the "ridge and runnel growth" described in the Geology section, page 17. Inlet site #2 on the site map points out the approximate location of the ocean inlet when the new land form was still an island. Again, similar to Clam Creek marsh, longshore currents closed off the ocean inlet leaving this marsh with only a sound inlet.

Different from the strong, regular tidal inundation to Clam Creek marsh, the inlet flow to this marsh is intermittently non-existent or weakly established. The inlet channel to this marsh may cut across the beach directly in front of the marsh, especially after a recent storm. In the weeks to follow, the inlet channel starts to meander. In a couple of months the inlet drifts westwardly where its flow may cross the beach in any number of locations going as far as half way to Clam Creek. Evidence of former channel crossings is seen in the water-filled pits and gullies among the fallen trees on the beach (see illustration below). Through the meandering process, the channel becomes so convoluted and the water flow so dissipated that it eventually fills in with sand, cutting off all tidal flow to the marsh. The marsh may not receive tidal flow for many months until a new channel is broken open by a storm. (Both of the the Jekyll Island maps show the tidal creek in its closed-off position.)

The presence of sea oxeye, salt meadow cordgrass, and numerous hammocks scattered throughout the marsh attest to its poor tidal circulation. Due to the periodic opening and closing of the inlet, the marsh creek has earned the name of "Sometimes Creek." A comparison of this marsh with the cordgrass-dominated Clam Creek marsh points out the importance of regular tidal flow to maintain the integrity of a salt marsh.

Large terraces of clay on the beach are often exposed by the meandering of this inlet channel. The clay is from the marsh when it occupied this area at a prior time. Many of the little pits and impressions in the clay are where plants and burrowing animals resided when this area was a marsh. Orange-red colors occasionally seen on the pit walls are iron oxide deposits produced by the occupants introducing oxygen into the *anaerobic* clay (see Glossary under *iron oxide* for a further explanation). The clay is excellent for making pottery.

Sea Oxeye

Following the channel across the beach offers opportunities to further study water-flow dynamics and its effects on sand formations. One such formation is the *delta*. On a lower tide, the inlet channel often flanges out into deltas close to where it enters the sound waters (see illustration). Watch the water and sand movement where the channel expands into a delta to see the processes involved in its formation (see *delta* in the Glossary for an explanation).

Site 3, page 72, mentioned a special form of *ripples*, called *antidunes*, which are often seen in this particular tidal channel because of its rapid

Delta

water flow. Under these conditions the bottom of the channel is usually sheared flat with occasional, isolated groups of mound-like ripples rising up from the bottom. These ripples may stay still or slowly migrate against the current, giving them their name, antidunes.[27] Often they peak high enough to tumble over like miniature breakers against the water flow just before they are whisked away by the running water. In another location of the channel a similar sequence occurs, each taking less than 30 seconds to go through its cycle. The description in the Glossary on *ripples* may be helpful in seeking an explanation for antidune behavior.

The speed of the water flow in the inlet channel also offers an excellent opportunity to observe meandering in motion. On the outer swings of the meanders the water undercuts the banks and the sand falls in. (Students often hear the splashing sounds of the sand hitting the water before they are aware of what is happening.) On the inner banks the sand rapidly accumulates. (The meandering process is diagrammed and described under *meandering* in the Glossary.)

Those on bicycles could cross the little inlet channel (if one is there at the time) and ride the mile-and-a-half-long ocean beach to Site 9. For those on foot, it is recommended that you return to your cars and motor to Site 9. An alternative route back to Clam Creek bridge could be made by following a path through the woods that parallels the beach. The entrance to the wooded path is close to the western edge of the second marsh. Shortly after entering the woods, you come across another path which goes south for about a mile into the woods and ends at a point on the ocean beach about 1/4 mile north from the North Beach Picnic Area. Those returning to their automobiles should stay on the path paralleling the beach.

The forest surrounding the path to the bridge is predominately live oak and pine with a palmetto-sparkle berry-red bay understory. A variety of woodpeckers are seen working on these weather-worn trees. The path rises and falls as it traverses the dune ridges that formed from this portion of Holocene upland. Some of the swales between the ridges are sloughs. As this book is being written, the beach has retreated to where one of the sloughs, closer to Clam Creek marsh, has now opened out onto the beach. This fairly new feature is an indicator that the entire path may end up on the beach in the not-so-distant future. At the approach to the Clam Creek bridge, the upper end of the macadam bike path that comes from the North Beach Picnic Area is passed. (More is mentioned about this path in Site 9.)

Pileated

Red Bellied

Flicker

Downey

Woodpeckers

~

The North Beach Picnic Area, Site 9, is about 1/2 mile southeast from the entrance to the Clam Creek Picnic Area on Beachview Drive. On the way to the picnic area, Beachview crosses over the southern tail of Clam Creek marsh. The North Area Site map shows the tail end of the marsh angling toward the south-west and cleaving deeply into the island. The red maples at the southern extreme of the marsh indicate the presence of a large freshwater slough which drains into the marsh from that end. The red maples are identified from afar by their red buds and red winged fruits in the late winter and spring, and red leaves in the fall. A foot path which traverses the upper reaches of the slough is found on Major Horton Road just past the pump station and pond (see North Area Site map).

Red Maple

SITE 9. North Beach Picnic Area

NATURAL HISTORY: Rapidly-eroding, boneyard beach and relic inlet sites on Jekyll's Holocene island fragment, a study and comparison of pine root structure with that of oaks in the severely eroded beach forests, and a diked bike path through Clam Creek marsh.

Around 1986 the North Beach Picnic Area was closed for renovations to mitigate erosion problems and to landscape the park. The artificial dunes among the live oaks and the northern extension of a loosely-bouldered (rip-rap) seawall are the products of this abandoned restoration project. It is surprising that these mounds of dirt have not smothered the root systems and killed the live oaks. Mother Nature somehow survives man's portrayals of nature.

After crossing over the weed-covered "dunes," walk north along the upper edge of the rip-rap seawall. This area is perhaps the most striking example of wind-sculptured oaks on the island. This area and the boneyard beach to the north are a photographer's paradise. Notice the differential growth patterns on the windward and the leeward sides of the trees. The windward limbs are many-branched and shrubbed, while those on the more protected side of the tree are fewer and longer. The trees closest to the beach are dwarfed and severely raked backward, while those in the more sheltered, back areas are larger and better developed. As the eye scans the tree tops, the beginning of a slanted *shearline* is perceived. Many of these same features are described in more detail in Site 2. (The Glossary, under *windshearing* and *shrubbing effect*, presents the mechanics which produce the wind-sculptured shapes described above.)

Wind-shorn oaks on the North Beach Picnic Area

Standing on the beach near the end of the rip-rap wall, the rate of retreat of the unprotected beach becomes apparent. The beach has retreated about 150 feet since this section of the rip-rap wall was erected nine years ago. Most of the trees that are now dead on the beach were alive and well in back of the intertidal zone at that time.

The clay terraces on this section of beach and areas further south are evidence of the existence of a marsh behind the Holocene island that fronted the entire North Area shoreline of Jekyll Island (see Geology, page 15).

For the next 2/10 mile north of the sea wall, the beach has been eroding and penetrating a live oak forest. Numerous examples of denuded singles and clusters of live oaks show their flat, spreading root systems. The clustered trees show how the roots entangle to form a strong support system against the wind, but alas, they offer little defense against the advancing sea.

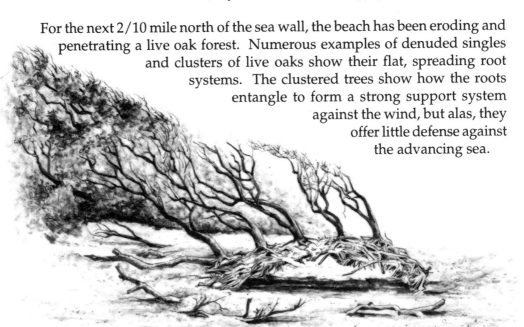

Peering back through the woods, one becomes aware of the closeness of Clam Creek marsh, on the other side of this strip of upland. This suggests that the ocean inlet to Clam Creek (inlet site #1 on the North Area Site map) was located somewhere along this section of live oak forest. Some long-time residents of Jekyll report that their grandparents used to crab at that inlet when it was still active. If erosion continues at its present rate, the marsh will eventually merge with the retreating beach, reopening the inlet; and once again the Holocene fragment will become an island.

Just north of the live oak beach is a beach fronted by a pine forest which is undergoing a similar erosion. Every stage of exposure of the pine trees and their roots can be seen on this beach. As can be observed, a pine may have one or several main tap roots directly below the trunk and smaller taps descending from radiating horizontal roots. From this we now see how the radiating root configurations seen on the North End Beach came from the roots of pines. With such a system of tap roots, each pine is well supported on its own. One can see from these standing, denuded trees that the exposed roots would be first to snap when a pine falls, leaving the roots in the sand (see illustration on the opposite page). The resinous pine, being highly buoyant and having a relatively small crown for the size of the tree, tends to float away in the storm -- accounting for why fallen pine trees are not often found on the beaches.

In contrast to pines, fallen oaks tend to remain on the beaches. The oaks stay intact as they fall over because of the relative ease with which their shallow roots are exposed and wrested out of the sand. The highly branching crown and roots become snagged and buried in the sand under the tree's immense weight. Because of the great strength of the dense wood, the limbs do not easily snap. With the wood's resistance to weathering and fungal attack, the fallen live oaks remain for decades to form the boneyard beaches.

Through aerial surveys, topological maps, and walking the North Beach, the ocean inlet to the smaller marsh (inlet site #2) appears to have occurred close to the northern end of this pine-fronted beach (see North Area Site map).

The beach above the pine forest is stable and fronted by small sea oat-covered dunes which periodically come and go with erosional fluctuations. This narrow beach with a steep slope and diminished meadow is characteristic of the rest of beach frontage to close to the vicinity of the northern tip of the island. The beach offers no special features to make the long trek to it worthwhile, but on a bicycle the ride is pleasant as long as the wind is at your back. Those on foot might at this point return to the picnic area.

Behind the beach close to the end of the rip-rap seawall there is an access road to Beachview Drive. The short distance from the beach to Clam Creek Marsh along this road reveals the narrowness of this end of the Holocene land fragment. An excellent view of Clam Creek Marsh from its southern end is seen from this road. The south end of a macadam bike path, which travels the entire length of Clam Creek marsh close to its eastern shore, is seen from this road. We saw the north end of the bike path when we returned to Clam Creek Bridge from the North End Beach in Site 8.

BIKE PATH

The bike path is slightly over a mile, again making a pleasant ride on a bicycle but a long walk for those on foot. Walking a short distance on the path from either end gives one a fairly good idea of what is encountered for the duration of the walk. The bike path was a road built on a dike with two culverts to allow tidal circulation to reach the entrapped marshes on the eastern side. In light of this, one might be surprised at the robust growth of cordgrass in that isolated, eastern segment of marsh. Light is shed on this mystery with the discovery of a number of areas where tidal-creek tributaries have eroded through the dike, creating their own "culverts." Such breakthroughs often lead to the collapse of the dike as revealed by the patches in the macadam.

In several places the bike path runs close to marsh hammocks. Walking into the hammocks is not advised because of the possibility of surprising a snake hidden in the leaf litter (see Safety and Health, Appendix E). Some of the hammocks closer to the northern end of the path have sufficient surrounding sandy (high) marsh to allow easy walking around them at a lower tide. The various zones of the marsh and border communities surrounding the hammocks become accessible for closer study. Fiddler crabs abound in these areas during the warmer months.

Sand Fiddler

Alligator slides, areas where grasses have been bent and pressed down by the bodies of alligators sliding into nearby watery areas, are seen along the path. Churring calls of kingfishers are often heard, directing the eye to these striking, cerulean birds with their over-sized heads. This is a popular bike path with island residents.

Belted Kingfisher

96

GLOSSARY

GLOSSARY OF TERMS AND CONCEPTS

The glossary defines and explains the meanings of italicized words used in the text. These pages are marked for quick location of this section. Some terms require only a short definition while others, which introduce concepts, may require several paragraphs with figures. Such explanations may occasionally spawn new vocabulary words and related concepts which go beyond the context of the terms being defined, but contribute to a deeper understanding of the subject matter covered in the text. Wherever possible, terms and concepts from other areas of the glossary are integrated into each definition and explanation.

New vocabulary words introduced in a definition or explanation are underlined. Technical vocabulary words from other areas of the glossary that are used in a definition or explanation are *italicized*. An underlined, italicized word appearing in a bracket after a definition or explanation is another term in the glossary that closely relates to the term being looked up, and often aids in its comprehension. Where a word has been taken from a specific area of the text, a reference to the text and page number is given in parentheses after the definition or explanation. The term *antidune* on this page provides an example of what is described in these last two sentences.

Accretion: to build by deposition. Beaches build up or grow by accretion of sand. An antonym of accretion is erosion.

Aerate: to place oxygen into an environment.

Aerobic: the presence of oxygen. Aerobic also describes an organism which requires oxygen to live.

Anaerobic: absence of oxygen. Anaerobic is an antonym of *aerobic*.

Antidune: mobile mound-like *ripples* formed in the sand under shallow, fast-moving water. Antidunes get their name by often migrating against the water current. [*ripples*] (Site 8, page 91)

Antlion: an insect of the order Neoroptera. The larval stage produces and lives in conical pits commonly found in dry-soil, waste areas and sand. The larvae are 1/4- to 1/2-inch long, and are voracious insectivores. (An illustration of their pits and a description of their ingenuous method of trapping and eating prey is described in Site 3.) The adults are totally different from their larval counterparts in that they are fragile, 1 1/2-inch-long flying forms, resembling a damselfly (a smaller representative of the dragonfly family). Unlike damselflies, the

Larva

antlion adult has distinct antennae, is a weak flyer, and is *nocturnal*. The adults of some species are pollen eaters while other species lack functional mouth parts and do not eat. Life for the adult is brief and centered on breeding -- the food needs are largely taken care of during the larval stage. (Site 3, page 70)

Adult

Arboreal: living in trees.

Beach renourishment: the pumping of dredge spoils onto a beach as a measure of combating beach erosion. (Ocean Beach, page 22)

Effects of renourishment on beaches Renourished beaches, with their sands mixed with *silt* and shells from the dredge spoils, are often a poor substitute for natural sand beaches. The fine silts occupy air spaces between the sand grains smothering myriads of tiny organisms that live among the sand grains (*psammon*). This robs shorebirds and other animals of a valuable food source. Silty beaches often become sufficiently compact and hard as to prevent sea turtles from digging nests for a year or more after renourishment.[25] If a natural beach does not remain in an area, then an artificial beach will not remain either. For this reason renourished beaches often require the construction of *groins* and other potentially damaging holding structures.

Bermuda high: an area of high pressure which settles over the Southeast for much of the summer. Being a *high-pressure cell*, the Bermuda high's winds rotate clockwise. Continental, frontal storms approaching from the west are often driven northward by the Bermuda high's rotating winds, so that this area of the Southeast is often bypassed. For much of the summer, the coastal lands have to depend on the capricious, local *convection storms* for most of their rainfall, which makes this area susceptible to drought. [*high-pressure cell*] (Physical Setting, page 10)

Bernoulli effect: the negative pressure created by a *fluid* flowing over a surface. The faster the fluid flow, the greater the reduction in pressure between the surface and the fluid. This negative pressure or partial vacuum is experienced when you feel drawn into a fast-moving truck or train that passes by. The lift on an airplane is created by the negative pressure of air flowing over the upper surface of its wings as the plane is propelled forward.

Bromeliads: tropical plants which mostly grow in trees as *epiphytes*. Some, such as the pineapple, grow in soil. Most bromeliads are in the form of a rosette of stiff, spiny leaves which form a cup to catch water (see tropical bromeliad illustration). The Spanish moss and ball moss are highly modified versions of the typical bromeliad. (Site 4, page 75)

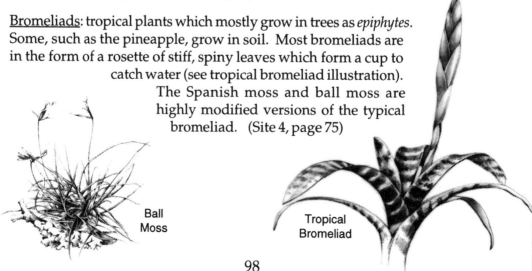

Ball
Moss

Tropical
Bromeliad

<u>Breakers</u>: waves which tumble over or break. The word used in this context centers on *translating waves* which break in shallow water and transport water toward the beaches (see glossary under *waves*).

1. <u>The process of wave breaking</u> As a wave moves into a shallow area, the subsurface part of the wave comes in contact with the bottom ("touches bottom"). Because of the frictional drag with the bottom, the lower part of the wave slows down, while the wave's crest continues at close to normal speed. The crest of the wave then moves ahead of the lower part and the wave tumbles over, becoming a breaker. Notice from Figure 20 that, as the waves enter the *critical depth* of water, their wave length is shortened and wave height increases. This happens because the faster moving waves coming from behind catch up with the slower moving waves in front. As wave length is shortened, the wave energy is compressed, which pushes up the wave height. And finally the wave energy is released explosively as the wave breaks.[26] [*waves*]

2. <u>Critical depth</u> is the depth of water in which a wave begins to break.
> CD (critical depth) = 2 x wave length, or
> CD = 1.3 x wave height

FIGURE 20: Diagram of a Breaking Wave

3. <u>Different types of breakers</u>

<u>Plunging breaker</u>: a fast-moving wave, whose crest is flung forward and falls to form a curl, which plunges powerfully into the water in front of the wave. The 25- to 30-foot waves ridden by surfers in California and Hawaii are supersized examples of these high-energy breakers.

<u>Spilling breaker</u>: a slower-moving wave whose crest collapses and tumbles down the wave slope as the breaker moves shoreward. Such low-energy breakers are more typical of the Georgia coast.

Buttress: expanded areas at the bases of trees which inhabit saturated soils. (Sloughs, page 45)

Canopy: the leafy crown of a tree. The canopies of many trees growing together may coalesce to form a canopy over the whole forest (forest canopy).

Climax community: a community of plants and animals which continues to propagate itself and tends to remain relatively unchanged over time under the prevailing environmental and climatic conditions. [succession]

Commensalism: a close, often intimate, relationship between two or more organisms in which one organism benefits, while the other(s) are not harmed or may also benefit. Commensalism is a form of Symbiosis.

Condensation of water: the change of water from a vapor to a liquid. When air cools, it compresses (becomes denser) and is unable to hold as much water in a vapor form. The excess water condenses into droplets which produce a mist or clouds. (Physical Setting, page 10)

Consumers: animals (and some plants) which consume living or dead organisms for nourishment (carnivores, herbivores, omnivores, etc.). [producers]

Continental shelf: the shallow undersea plain bordering a continent. It is often the submerged portion of a coastal plain. (Geology, page 13)

Continental slope: the outer edge of the continental shelf. The continental slope is often considered the perimeter of the continent. At the slope the terrain steeply declines often forming the wall of a submarine canyon. (Geology, page 13)

Convection currents: vertical, circular movements of a fluid (air or water) responding to differences in temperature and density. In the case of air rising over land during the day: the air is heated, decreases in density, and, like a helium-filled balloon, rises. Much of the surrounding air is drawn into these rising convection cells of heated air. Such thermal convections move large masses of air and moisture into the upper atmosphere. The reverse happens when the air is cooled. (Physical Setting, page 10) (Salt Marsh, page 38)

Convection storms: storms created by convection currents. (Physical Setting, page 10)

Cross bedding: the horizontal banding patterns of different sediments seen in a cross section of a beach (see illustration). They are positioned much like the

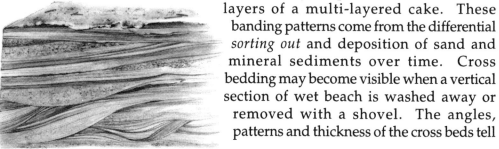

layers of a multi-layered cake. These banding patterns come from the differential sorting out and deposition of sand and mineral sediments over time. Cross bedding may become visible when a vertical section of wet beach is washed away or removed with a shovel. The angles, patterns and thickness of the cross beds tell

Cut-away view showing cross bedding

the geologist (sedimentologist) much about the direction and speed of water movement over the area where they were formed, and they reflect past erosional or *accretionary* events. Most geology texts go into detail on analysis of cross bedding (see Bibliography under Fritz[27]). [*sorting out of sediments*]

Decomposers: organisms which break down *organic matter* in the decaying process. Small animals, such as insects, worms, nematodes and protozoa in the soils and water, consume dead animals and other organic waste for nourishment. By passing through the myriad digestive systems of these organisms, complex organic products are sequentially reduced into simpler organic compounds, carrying out the gradual process of decomposition. The ultimate decomposers are the bacteria and fungi which break down the organic matter into *inorganic salts*.

Delta: the triangular-shaped extension of a tidal channel where it flows into a larger body of water. The term, tidal channel, may describe an inlet channel or a small tidal rivulet running off a beach (illustrated below). There are many kinds of deltas, so this definition and the following explanation are strictly confined to tidal channels.

The process of delta formation As a tidal channel approaches the sound or ocean, the depth of flow becomes sufficiently shallow so that the friction of the moving water with the bottom creates a *turbulent* flow. In a turbulent flow, water molecules tend to zig-zag causing the water to swing sideways at angles to the main flow. The water flow is then dissipated into progressively, smaller, branching channels and *rills*. The main and smaller branching channels also *meander*, further dissipating the flow. The overall result is a delta. As the flow decreases to a creep, the differential deposition (*sorting out*) of sediments becomes evident by the separation of the denser black minerals from the sand along the surface of the delta. (Site 8, page 91)

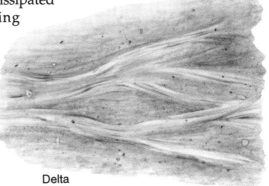

Delta

Desiccate: to become dry. Usually refers to the dehydration of living tissue.

Detritus: decomposed animal and plant matter that has been milled to a sediment through the movement of water and sand. At times there may be an abundance of a particular source-material supplying the detritus. For instance, cordgrass *wrack* coming from the marshes is eventually milled into a coffee-ground-like plant detritus which is deposited by the *longshore currents* along the high-tide lines and in wet, ripple troughs on the beaches. Fecal pellets from abundant ghost shrimp burrows on a beach frequently produce a muddy, fecal detritus which can coat large areas of wet sand in low-energy beaches, and is often seen in wet ripple depressions. These slimy, fecal-detritus deposits can be very slippery.

Diurnal: the active period of an animal occurring during the day. Diurnal is an antonym of *nocturnal*.

Dune ridge: *upland* ridges originally formed from sand dunes on relic beaches.

Ebb tide: a low tide. Ebb tide is the antonym of *flood tide*.

Ecosystem: biological communities existing in a specific physical environment. Pond ecosystem and beach-meadow ecosystem are examples.

Eddy currents: circular currents. Eddies are created when a *fluid* flow becomes *turbulent*. Anything that interrupts the flow of a moderately, fast-moving fluid creates eddies. Eddies are commonly seen when a paddle is pulled through water or when water flows past a piling.

Estuary: a body of water where sea water and fresh water mix. Sounds, marsh creeks and tidally-active ends of mainland rivers are examples of estuarine areas. (Salt Marsh, page 30)

Resurrection Fern

Epiphytes: plants that grow on trees and are completely independent of the soil. Spanish moss, resurrection fern, and the type of lichen illustrated are examples. [*bromeliad*]   (Site 4, page 75)

Lichen

Fallow: soil which is cleared, plowed, and then left unattended.   (Site 2, page 68)

Spanish moss

Feral: an introduced or domesticated animal that has become wild.

Flood tide: a high tide. Flood tide is an antonym of *ebb tide*.

Fluid: a liquid or gas. A fluid can be defined as the two physical states of matter, a gas and a liquid, which flow and conform to the shape of their containers. For our purposes, fluid is used in regard to water or air.

Fluting (flutes): vertical ridges or furrows on the *buttressed* areas of tree trunks. Fluting commonly occurs with cypress and buttonwood.   [*buttress*] (Slough, page 45)

Greenhouse gases: gases in the atmosphere which retain heat. Carbon dioxide (CO_2), methane, chlorofluorocarbon (CFC's), and nitrous oxide are examples of greenhouse gases. Similar to a greenhouse, these gases allow penetration and the escape of light and other solar energy, but retain some of the heat. Such heat retention accumulates over time and contributes to the global rise in atmospheric temperature. Global temperature increases, though slight, have devastating effects on the world's climate patterns and cause the sea level to rise through the melting of the ice caps. CO_2 is particularly influential in the greenhouse effect, not because it is more potent than the other gases, but because there is so much of it being added to the atmosphere through the burning of fossil fuels. (Geology, page 17)

Groins (jetties): walls constructed perpendicularly to the shoreline which trap sand moving in the *longshore currents* for the purpose of building a beach. Jetties are large groins.

Effect of groins on beaches   As the water approaches and courses around the groin, it is forced to slow down and change its direction of flow causing much of the suspended sand to be deposited on the side of the groin receiving the current (up-current side). On the way around the groin, some of the water is jetted off the end, carrying with it some of the remaining sand into the deeper waters outside of the *longshore current.* The longer the groin and/or the greater the speed of the current, the more sand is lost in this manner. Besides being bereft of sand, the directional changes made by the *turbulent* waters on the other side of the groin contribute to the down-current erosion. Depending on their size, groins and jetties can cause erosion to thousands of feet of down-current shoreline. As of this writing, five states have banned the construction of groins and jetties because of their damage to beaches.   (Ocean Beach, page 22)

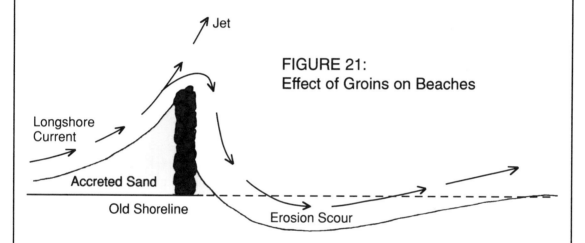

FIGURE 21:
Effect of Groins on Beaches

Groundwater: describes any underground source of water from deep water aquifers to standing shallow water creating wetlands. Groundwater accumulated from rain is the principal source of water available to the plants and animals of Coastal Georgia. (See *water table* in the Glossary for factors affecting groundwater retention and fluctuation in the soil.)   [*water table*]

Habitat: the local environment inhabited by a particular species.

Halophyte: a plant that inhabits highly *saline* or alkaline soils. (Salt Marsh, page 33)

Hammock: an island in a marsh.

High pressure cell: a large air mass whose winds rotate in a clockwise direction and are usually associated with clear weather. Low pressure cells: have counterclockwise-circulating winds and are usually associated with storms. [*Bermuda High*]   (Physical Setting, page 10)

Holocene Epoch: the time period from about 11,000 years ago to present. This is also considered the modern period. Holocene islands are barrier islands that have formed since the fourth and last great "Ice Age."   [*Pleistocene Epoch*] (Geology, page 15)

Humus: decaying plant and animal matter in the soil. Through the action of *decomposers*, humus supplies *inorganic* fertilizers for the plants growing in the soil and allows better water retention.   (Ocean Beach, page 28)

Inertia: the resistance of a stationary object to being moved, or the resistance of a moving object to change in speed, acceleration, or direction.

Inlet: an opening through which ocean waters enter and leave an enclosed body of water, such as a sound, bay, or marsh.

Inorganic salt: a compound formed from the chemical union of a metal and a non-metal (or radical), i.e., magnesium chloride, iron oxide, sodium phosphate, and hundreds of other mineral salts.* Among those beneficial to plants are nitrates, phosphates, and potassium salts.
   *Metals, non-metals, and radicals require chemical definitions and a periodic table which are found in any elementary chemistry text.

Intertidal: covered by water during high tide and exposed during low tide.

Iron oxide: the chemical union of iron with oxygen. In the case of the iron oxide production in the marsh soils, many burrowing animals, such as clams, worms, fiddler crabs, ghost shrimp, etc., introduce oxygen into their burrows through circulating seawater. Cordgrass *aerates* marsh soils by transporting oxygen to its roots. Where the marsh soil comes in contact with the oxygen, the black-colored iron sulfides in the *anaerobic* clay chemically combine with the oxygen forming the red-colored iron oxides. (Site 8, page 91)

Laminar flow: occurs when the molecules of a fluid and suspended particles move in the same direction as the fluid flow. Laminar flow usually occurs with slower moving fluids. When fluid flow speed or friction is increased beyond a certain critical point, the particles move erratically at angles to the overall flow, producing a *turbulent flow*.   [*turbulent flow*]

FIGURE 22: Laminar and Turbulent Flow

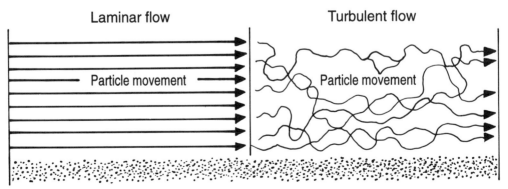

104

<u>Longshore currents</u>: local ocean currents that move parallel to the beaches within the *surf zone*. They are caused by wind and waves.

<u>Lowlands</u>: low-lying lands that have a potential for becoming saturated with rainfall or tidal inundation. Lowlands become *wetlands* when they characteristically retain water for longer periods of time. Lowland is the antonym of *upland*. [*wetland*]

<u>Meandering</u>: the winding of a river or creek.

1. <u>Meandering process</u> This occurs whenever there is a bend in a marsh creek, *inlet* or river. As the water flows around the curve, it tends to move faster on the outside of the turn and slower on the inside. The faster-moving water tends to erode the outer part of the turn, while the slower-moving water deposits sediments on the inner part called a <u>point bar</u> (see Figure 23). Point bars are the foundation on which new marsh land is formed. As Figure 24 shows, the curves in a tidal creek tend to become more exaggerated as this process continues.

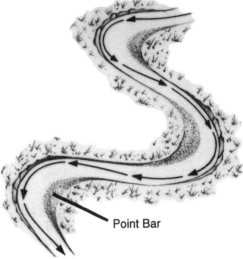

FIGURE 23: Direction of Water Movement in a Meandering Creek

2. <u>Oxbow formation</u> As a curve of a marsh creek erodes outward forming a loop, the curves at the base of the loop tend to erode inward toward each other. Eventually the two curves at the base of the loop may connect, breaking open a new and shorter pathway for water to flow. Seeking the path of least resistance, the major flow then takes place in the new pathway, and the longer loop is eventually bypassed. Figure 24 illustrates this process. Water stranded in these loops forms temporary ponds called oxbows, which eventually silt in with marsh sediments. Old marsh creeks often leave aside many oxbows as they flow their tortuous routes making new oxbows on the way. The North Area Site map, shows two oxbows formed by Clam Creek (Figure 17, page 61).

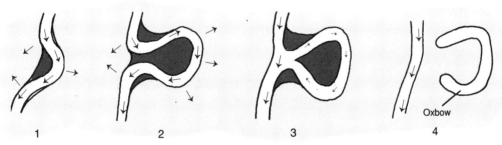

FIGURE 24: Meandering Process and Oxbow Formation in a Tidal Creek

▨ Sediments Deposited

→ Direction of Erosion

→ Water Flow

<u>Neretic</u>: pertains to shallow oceans near the continents.   [*pelagic*]

<u>New World</u>: native to North and South America.   (Site 3, page 74)

<u>Nocturnal</u>: active at night. Nocturnal is an antonym of *diurnal.*

<u>Old World</u>: native to Asia, Africa, and Europe.   (Site 3, page74)

<u>Organic matter</u>: compounds made up of carbon chains, such as proteins, carbo-hydrates, lipids, nucleic acids, etc. Life forms are composed of organic compounds.

<u>Osmosis</u>: diffusion of water from an area of higher concentration of water through a <u>differentially permeable</u> membrane to an area of lower water concentration. Most living membranes freely diffuse water, but the passage of other materials, such as dissolved salts and *organic matter*, pass through more slowly or not at all, hence the name differentially permeable. Increased salt in an aquatic environment lowers the water concentration. When the *salinity* of an environment abruptly increases, organisms whose tissues were osmotically balanced with their surroundings may become dehydrated because of water lost to the environment through diffusion. Conversely, when salinity is lowered, water concentration of the environment is increased. The increased water diffusion into the tissues causes cells to expand and, in extreme cases, explode. If an organism lacks physiological capabilities to counteract such osmotic changes or is unable to escape them, they are subject to <u>osmotic death</u>.   (Salt Marsh, Page 32)

<u>Oxbow</u>: stranded ponds formed by the meandering process.   [*meandering*]

<u>Oxidation</u>: the chemical union of oxygen with another element or compound. (Oxidation is also the gaining of electrons through a chemical reaction. This form of oxidation is explained in an elementary chemistry text.)

   1. <u>Rapid oxidation</u> takes place when oxygen quickly combines with substances. Rapid oxidation usually produces heat and in many instances fire, such as with the burning of wood.

   2. <u>Slow oxidation</u> is the gradual oxidation that takes place with the oxygen in the air or dissolved oxygen in water at normal environmental temperatures. Because of the reactive nature of oxygen, slow oxidation takes place at all times with any substance with which oxygen can react. This is especially true of organic waste (i.e. feces, secretion products, *detritus*, dead organisms, and other non-living *organic matter*).   In cases where there is too much organic waste matter in poorly-circulated ponds or flooded marsh areas, slow oxidation can rob sufficient dissolved oxygen to cause the animal life in those systems to suffocate and die. Fish-kills resulting from oxygen depletion occasionally occur in nature and many times they are associated with human pollution. (Salt Marsh, page 31)

<u>Parasitism</u>: a *symbiotic* relationship where one organism benefits (parasite) at the expense of the other (host) which is damaged from the relationship.

<u>Pelagic</u>: pertains to the open ocean.   [*neretic*]

Plankton: suspended life that drifts with the ocean currents (zooplankton are animals, phytoplankton are plants and algae). (Salt Marsh, page 37)

Pleistocene Epoch: the time period extending from about 1 million to about 11 thousand years ago. During this period great glaciers advanced and retreated over the temperate regions of the world, dividing this period of time into four major "Ice Ages." Georgia's Pleistocene islands formed before the fourth and last Ice Age over this period of time. [Holocene Epoch] (Geology, page 13).

Pocket marsh: a marsh almost completely surrounded by uplands and having one tidal inlet. Both Clam Creek marsh and the small marsh near the tip of North End Beach are examples of pocket marshes.

Producers: the organisms that manufacture organic matter. The vast amount of production is done through photosynthesis by green plants and algae. [consumers]

Psammon: tiny creatures living in the water suspended between sand grains under the surface of a wet beach. (Ocean Beach, Page 24)

Recurved spits: elongated spits growing from the southern ends of barrier islands. Uplands originating from recurved spits are formed from the rows of dune ridges left behind by a southerly growing shoreline. The southern ends of barrier islands are often formed from recurved spits, as is the case with the lower one-third of Jekyll Island. (Geology, page 17)

Refraction (light refraction): the bending and separating of light into its respective colors from its passage through crystals or other transparent substances of different densities. Light refraction often produces rainbows. Various refractory substances tend to refract particular spectra of the rainbow emitting specific colors. The web of the golden silk spider refracts a gold color. Birds with metallic sheens have feathers which refract a variety colors, for example: the purple and copper colors of blackbirds, the metallic blues and greens of a peacock, and the blue, green and purple wing patches of ducks. One can determine whether the color of a feather is produced by light refraction or by a pigment by looking through the feather at a light source. The refracted colors disappear, while the pigmented colors remain. (Site 1, page 64) (Site 7, page 88)

Refraction (wave refraction): the change in direction of a water wave in response to varying frictional forces along its length.

   Wave refraction process As a wave approaches a shallow area, the part of the wave that reaches the shallows first is slowed down by the friction of the wave movement with the bottom. The part of the wave in the deeper water continues to move at close to the original speed. The faster moving part of the wave swings around toward the slower moving areas, in much the same way a bulldozer turns toward the side where the caterpillar treads are braked. Wave refraction occurs as waves swing around a curved shore line (see Figure 10, page 17). This process ultimately causes incoming waves to become more parallel to the beachfront regardless of their original angle of approach. (Site 7, page 89).

Rill: a small stream of water or rivulet.   [_delta_]

Ripples: regularly raised areas in the sand (or soil) formed by the movement of fluid (air or water) over its surface. Ripples formed by fluid flow and water waves are considered below.

Formation of fluid-flow ripples   As fluid (air or water) moves over sand, a decreased or negative pressure is created at the surface of the sand (see _Bernoulli effect_). If the flow is sufficiently fast, sand grains (and minerals) are sucked up into moving fluid and are carried for a distance. If the fluid flow is not too fast, the grains will eventually drop out because the Bernoulli effect that drew them up is neutralized as the grains move with the fluid. Once settled, the movement of the fluid over the stationary grains again creates the negative surface pressure and once again the grains are drawn up into current. Often sand grains dropping down dislodge or "kick up" other grains near the points of impact. Under a fairly steady fluid flow, this jumping pattern of particles becomes regular (rhythmic) and is known as saltation. The average distance traveled by the sand grains during saltation dictates the spacing of the ripples. Up to a critical velocity, the faster the fluid movement the larger and wider apart the ripples.[27]

FIGURE 25: Saltation of Sand Grains
(Adopted from Fritz)[27]

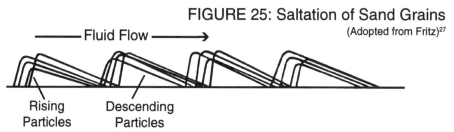

Coarser particles have shorter saltation distances and may bounce many times while moving along the length of a ripple. Particles that are too heavy for saltation, often roll or slide up the gentle slope (stross) of the ripples, through a behavior known as surface creep, and end up on the ripple crests with the saltating particles. When a critical mass of particles accumulates on the crests, the particles avalanche down the steep slip face, and then commence moving up the slope of the next ripple in response to the fluid flow (see Figure 26).[27] Through the above processes, ripples grow and migrate with the current. Watching this process, especially in wind-driven sand, one is impressed by the blur of bouncing, creeping and tumbling of sand grains as the rows of ripples glide in flanking formation over the sand surface. (Many of the events described above apply to the growth and movement of _sand dunes_).   [_sorting out of sediments_] [_sand dunes_]   (Site 3, page 73)

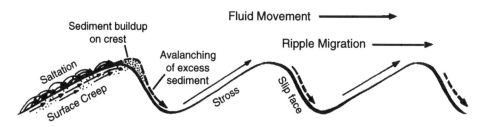

FIGURE 26: Movements of Coarser Particles along Ripple Faces

Formation of wave-formed ripples   As volleys of small, wind-driven wavelets move over shallow waters, the gentle oscillation of the water alternately scours and redeposits sand with a rhythmic, swishing movement to form symmetrical ripples (see Figure 27). Figure 33, page 116, is helpful in understanding Figure 27, because it shows the relationship of the surface waves to the circular movement of the water below and the movements of the sea grass on the bottom. The forces that produce the rhythmic swaying of the sea grass are the same as those creating the symmetrical ripples.   [*waves*] (Site 3, page 72)

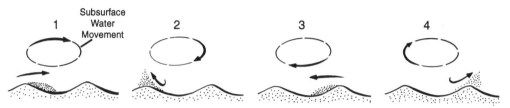

FIGURE 27: Process of Wave Produced Ripples
(Modified from Fritz) [27]

If the water remains stationary as described in the previous paragraph, the resultant ripples become symmetrical. If the water is moving, the resultant ripples become more asymmetrical as fluid-flow factors interact with the wave processes.   (Site 3, page 72)

———— Water Flow ———→

Symmetrical Ripples   Asymmetrical Ripples

Runnel: gullies on the wet *intertidal* beach which run approximately parallel to the shore line. Runnels often develop where sand carried by waves from off-shore shoals meets the sand on the beach. Runnels often act as channels through which *ebbing* tide waters flow back to the sea.   (Ocean Beach, page 22)

Saline: containing salt, salty.

Salinity: salt concentration.

Salt pruning: dehydration of tree limbs, buds, and leaves by the salt carried in sea breezes. Droplets of salt water are thrown into the air by the surf spray, wave action, and by the popping of sea foam bubbles. The droplets are carried inland by the sea breezes and are deposited on the exposed parts of plants. The water evaporates, leaving the salt which *osmotically* draws out water killing plant tissues. Surprisingly, the popping bubbles are the most far-reaching cause of salt destruction, because the fine, "atomized" droplets travel for miles.[28] [*wind shearing* and *shrubbing effect*]

Sand bars: elongated *shoals* which parallel the beach. They are formed at a point close to where the breakers crash (see *surf zone* for details). The larger the waves, the larger and further out the sand bar. If there are several sizes of wave trains moving in the surf zone, there may be several sand bars running parallel to the beach. [shoals] [surf zone] (Ocean Beach, page 21)

Sand dune: large *ripple*-like elevations of sand. Different than ripples, sand dunes are usually large, singular formations that may be 1 to 100 feet high.

Formation, growth and migration of sand dunes Wind-formed sand dunes usually have their origin with some object lying on the beach which interrupts the surface wind flow. As the air passes over the object, it increases its velocity to stay up with surrounding air flowing over the sand surface. The increased rate of air flow and the resistance to its having to flow over the obstruction creates a localized area of reduced air pressure on the top and the leeward side of the object (see *Bernoulli effect*). The lowered pressure separates the air flow which creates *eddy currents* on the lee side. If the wind speed is sufficient to carry sand, the eddy currents trap the sand on the top and leeward side of the object, eventually burying it and creating a sand dune. A sand dune is typically asymmetrical with its gradually-sloped stross windward to the steeper slip face. With continued sand deposition and accumulated sand avalanching down the slip face, the dune grows and migrates with the wind. Figure 28 diagrams the above descriptions. Also see Figure 26 under *ripples* in the Glossary because the description of the movements of coarse particles over the surface of ripples closely applies to particle-movement patterns over sand dunes. [*ripples*]

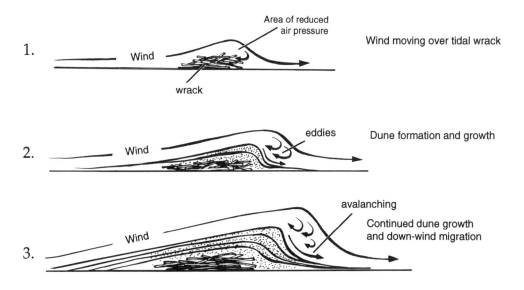

FIGURE 28: Growth and Migration of a Sand Dune
(Modified from Fritz)[27]

Saprophyte: a plant which lives on decaying *organic matter* in the soil. Such plants often lack the green pigment, chlorophyll, and do not photosynthesize. Coral-root is an example. (Maritime Forest, page 41)

<u>Seawalls</u>: vertical or slanted walls constructed parallel to the shoreline to protect beachfront property from being eroded by wave action.

<u>Effect of seawalls on beaches</u> Seawalls are built to protect beachfront property, but such structures often cause beaches to disappear. The energy of the waves breaking against the wall is concentrated on the beach immediately in front of the wall, scouring away the sand. Loss of sand from the beach close to the wall lowers the beach profile. This causes the sand further down the beach to become unstable and to wash away. Because of the beach's lowered elevation, larger waves break further up the beach, exacerbating erosion even during clement weather. The sand reservoir in the dune fields and meadows behind the wall is blocked from taking part in the sand sharing system, which, as we learned, is so vital to preservation of the beach (see Ocean Beach, pages 21 and 22). In most cases this degrading cycle continues until the beach washes away. The loss of sand and the scouring action of the waves can expose the seawall's underpinnings, taking away its support and eventually causing it to sink or fall apart. Figure 29 depicts the above descriptions. Thousands of miles of America's beaches have been lost to seawalls.[5] (Ocean Beach, page 22)

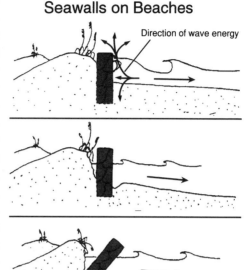

FIGURE 29: Effects of Seawalls on Beaches

Direction of wave energy

⟶ Net movement of sand

<u>Shearline</u>: the backward-slanting profile of a forest *canopy* caused by the shearing action of wind and salt spray (see Figure 19, page 66). [*wind shearing*]

<u>Shoals</u>: underwater bodies of sand which become exposed during low tide.

<u>Shrubbing effect</u>: the growth of many short, scraggly limbs in wind-blown trees, especially those close to the beach. The shrubbing effect is best understood with a brief explanation of the relationship between buds and limb growth. The <u>terminal bud</u> at the end of a limb normally inhibits the growth of the nearest <u>lateral buds</u>. The lateral buds are located just above where the leaf stalks attach to the stem. As the limb grows in length, the terminal bud becomes further from the older lateral buds and its inhibitory influence diminishes. The lateral buds then grow and produce new branching stems. As the main stem continues to grow, more of the lateral buds become free of the tip dominance and grow. This is nature's ways of eliminating excessive competition among too many lateral limbs and their leaves. Because of the tip dominance, the limbs become longer and the entire tree more graceful in appearance than those impacted by winds.

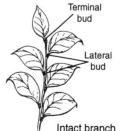

Terminal bud

Lateral bud

Intact branch

In forests assaulted by sea breezes, the terminal buds that grow beyond the protective canopy are killed by the desiccating winds and salt, which unleashes premature growth of all the lateral buds on the stem. Each branch formed by the lateral buds has its own terminal and lateral buds, and many of these are affected in the same way, making the wind-exposed trees or parts of trees smaller and shrubbier. The same shrubbing effect is achieved when bushes around the house are regularly trimmed. [*wind shearing*] [*salt pruning*]

Terminal bud removed

Growth of lateral buds
after loss of terminal bud

Silt: a fine sediment of mud or clay.

Slack tide: when tidal movement stops at maximum high or low tides.

Sorting out of sediments: various darker-colored minerals and sand move differentially under the influence of wind and water currents. The mineral particles are both smaller and denser than the sand grains. Their small size gives the minerals less surface area to be drawn up into the moving air or water flow above them, and their greater density causes the suspended mineral particles to drop out of the flow sooner; so minerals do not travel as far or as fast as the sand (see *ripples*). The minerals, then, tend to settle at the base of the ripples while the sand migrates further up the ripple slope and deposits on the crests and the leeward sides. Larger particles (coarser sand, shell fragments, detritus, etc.) tend to roll or slide along the sand surface and these also tend to collect in the ripple troughs. Besides density and size of sediments, other factors, such as particle shape and cohesiveness, affect the sorting process along ripple surfaces. With the accumulation of sand over time, this differential sorting process produces *cross bedding*. [*ripples*] [*cross bedding*] (Site 3, page 72)

Specific heat of water: the quantity of heat (calories) required to raise one gram of water one degree centigrade. Water has a high specific heat in comparison to air, soil and rocks. In other words, it takes a longer time for a body of water to change its temperature in response to changing air temperature than does the land. The water's resistance to temperature change is why coastal lands or lands near large lakes experience less temperature change from night to day and throughout the seasons than lands remote from water. Another way to look at this is that coastal lands are heated or cooled by the near-by waters during atmospheric temperature changes. This is why the temperatures of the Georgia coast are more moderate than those further inland.
 (Physical Setting, page 10)

Spits: *shoals* which are attached to an island or mainland shore.

Storm surge: a rise in water level due to a low barometric pressure associated with a storm. Tropical depressions such as hurricanes often have exceedingly low barometric pressures (hence, the term depression) which create high storm surges. The Hurricane of 1898 arrived on the Georgia coast during a high spring tide. Adding the storm surge and the strong winds driving the water into the coast at a high tide, an overall 25-foot elevation of water was created which covered many of the islands and put Brunswick under 6 feet of water.

112

Subtidal: below the *intertidal* level. Except for unusually low tides and strong land breezes, subtidal zones remain under water throughout the tidal cycle.

Succession (plant succession): sequential changes in plant communities that accompany changes in the physical environment (soil, climate, etc.). Subsequent improvements in the physical environment enables more demanding and competitive plant species to be supported. The more aggressive plants eventually take over the *habitats* bringing about changes in the plant community. Plant communities may undergo many changes (successional stages) in response to continued changes in the physical environment until a *climax community* becomes established. In somewhat the same manner, changes in animal communities respond to changes in a physical environment (animal succession). Ecological succession is a term embracing both animal and plant succession.

Surf zone: the zone between the breaking waves and the wave-wash on the beach. Wave-induced currents work like a conveyer belt where foaming water thrust by breakers moves along the surface of the water until it washes onto the beach. Water from the beach is drawn back toward the rising breakers in a current below the incoming water, sometimes referred to as the "undertow." The outgoing water is drawn up into breaking waves to again be transported to the beach. As the water undergoes its 180-degree directional change, its movement is temporarily reduced and some of the suspended sand carried in the water falls out just before the breaker tumbles (see Figure 30). In this way deposits from wave after wave build up to form a *sand bar*. Depending on the size of the waves and the slope of the beach, the surf zone may vary from hundreds of feet long with several trains of breakers to breakers that crash directly onto the exposed beach. The location of the surf zone and associated sand bars varies with the tides, seasonal wind and wave patterns, and storm episodes. [*sand bars*]   (Ocean Beach, page 21)

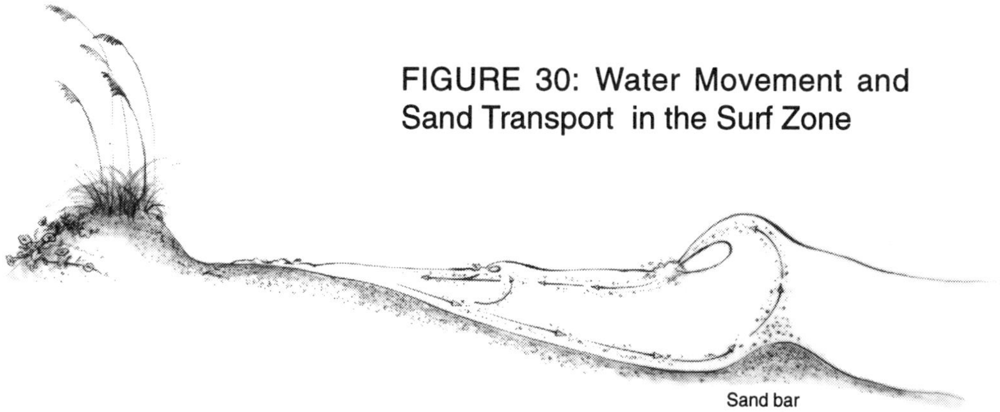

FIGURE 30: Water Movement and Sand Transport in the Surf Zone

Sand bar

Swale: a low area between dune ridges.

Swamp: a *wetland* area supporting lowland forests. Cypress swamps, bay swamps, gum and red maple ponds are examples of Georgia coastal swamps. Swamps support trees as opposed to marshes which support mainly grasses. (Freshwater Sloughs, page 45)

Symbiosis: two or more organisms living in close association with each other. *Commensalism* and *parasitism* are examples.   (Site 4, page 76)

Tabby: a concrete-like substance made by mixing equal parts of lime, whole shells, sand and water. These substances are mixed to form a slurry which is poured into a mold and allowed to set. The lime is made from oyster shells which are cooked or burned until they become crumbly and then they are crushed into a granular lime. Tabby structures are surprising resistant to weathering as so many of the well-preserved ruins attest.   (Major Horton House, page 85)

Tides: daily fluctuation of the sea level caused by gravitational attraction of the sun and the moon. The strength of the gravitational pull is a function of both the size and the distance between the bodies sharing the gravity. Even though the moon is far smaller than the sun, it is significantly closer to the earth causing it to have almost twice the tide-generating force as that of the sun.

$$Gravity = \frac{Mass_1 \times Mass_2}{Distance^2}$$

The equation shows that distance is in an exponential relationship with gravity causing it to have a far greater influence than those of the masses.

The tidal pull affects all of the earth, but the only part of the earth that visibly responds to the pull is water, because it is a liquid. The area of water directly under the moon or sun is drawn up into a bulge by gravitational attraction. Areas not under the gravitational forces become depressions relative to the bulges (see Figure 32). The bulges remain under the sun and moon as the earth makes its daily rotation. The shorelines which slip under the bulges experience a high tide, and those under the depressions a low tide. There are numerous factors that affect tidal periods and ranges -- most earth science and oceanography texts cover these. We have already seen how the shape of a continent, low barometric pressure, and high onshore winds can affect tides (see Physical Setting, page 11 and *storm surge* in the Glossary). Two other factors that need explanation are semidiurnal tides and spring and neap tides.

1. Semidiurnal tides two high tides and two low tides each day. Figure 32 shows that there is a tidal bulge of equal magnitude on the side of the earth opposite the pull of gravity for both the sun and the moon. For students studying tides, the presence of the force opposite the gravitational force is often perplexing. To simplify the explanation, let us consider alone the most dominant tidal force, the moon. The moon is said to orbit the earth, but actually both the moon and earth orbit about a common axis. In this way the gravitational attraction between the earth and the moon is balanced by the outward-thrusting, centrifugal force generated by their circling about the axis (see Figure 31).

Since the earth is many times the mass of the moon, the earth's center is much closer to the common axis of rotation than that of the moon's. The earth's orbit, then, is more like a wobble compared to the wide arc of the moon's path.

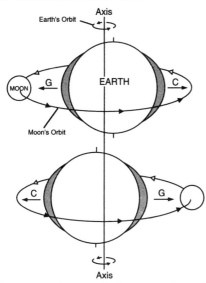

FIGURE 31: Tides Produced by Gravitational and Centrifugal Forces between the Earth and the Moon.

G - Pull of Gravity
C - Centrifugal Force
▨ - Tidal Bulge

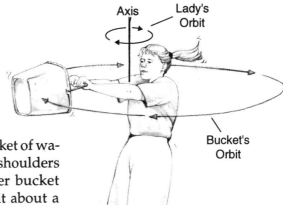

This is similar to a lady swinging a bucket of water in a circle. The lady's head and shoulders move in a small arc while the lighter bucket swings in a full arc as they both orbit about a common axis. Notice that the lady's ponytail swings outward because of the centrifugal force imparted to the back of her head. Likewise, a centrifugal force is imparted to the side of the earth opposite the pull of gravity. This centrifugal force creates the second tidal bulge which is equal and opposite the one caused by gravity.

2. <u>Spring and Neap tides</u> tidal extremes created by the relative positions of the sun and moon. Spring tides, the highest tides, occur twice a month when the moon and sun are in alignment during the new and full moons. Figure 32 shows that during these times, the gravitational forces of the sun and moon add to each other, increasing the differences between the high and low tides. Neap tides occur between spring tides when the sun and moon are at 90-degree angles to each other during the quarter moons. The figure shows that the water attracted by the sun and moon occur at different quarters of the globe, so that the differences between the high and low tides are at its lowest point, causing the neap tide. The magnitude of the tides gradually changes between these spring- and neap-tide extremes as the moon moves in its 27 1/3-day lunar orbit around the earth. A tide table reveals the regular rise and fall of the tidal heights in each two-week cycle.

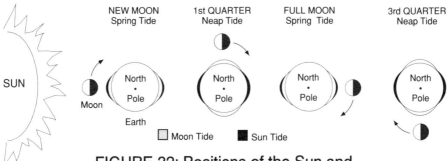

FIGURE 32: Positions of the Sun and Moon during Spring and Neap Tides

<u>Turbid</u>: waters clouded with suspended matter. (Salt Marsh, page 37)

<u>Turbulent flow</u> (turbulence): a flow (usually shallow or fast-moving) where the movement of the fluid molecules and suspended particles becomes erratic and moves at angles to the direction of the flow (See *laminar flow*, Figure 22). Turbulence greatly increases the friction of fluid movement and is often accompanied by *eddy currents*. Turbulent flow deviates from a laminar flow where the fluid particles and suspended materials move uniformly in the same direction as the fluid as seen in slower moving flows. [*laminar flow*]

<u>Uplands</u>: well-drained lands whose ground surface is above the *water table* and above normal tidal inundation. Uplands are an antonym of *lowlands*.

<u>Water table</u>: the upper level of *groundwater* accumulated from rains and other sources of surface water. In coastal Georgia, underground clay layers block further penetration of rain water through the soil causing a source of subsurface groundwater to accumulate above the clay layers. When these clay layers are close to the surface of the ground, the water table is frequently exposed, creating a wetland. In the barrier islands, the depth of the water table below the ground surface is dependent on the amount of rainfall, so its level fluctuates with dry and wet seasons. [*groundwater*] (Slough, page 45)

<u>Waves</u> (water waves): movement of energy in the form of crests and troughs through the surface layers of water.

  1. <u>Oscillatory waves</u> are waves that move through the water but do not transport water with their movement. As the waves pass over the surface, the water, down to about twice the wave's length, rotates in circular orbits. Objects on the bottom of shallow areas reflect the water movement by moving back and forth. An object floating on the water surface moves up and down with the passing crests and troughs with no appreciable gain in distance. Figure 33 illustrates the above descriptions. (The Glossary under *ripples* describes and illustrates how oscillartory waves create symmetrical, wave-formed ripples on a shallow, sandy bottom. [*ripples*]

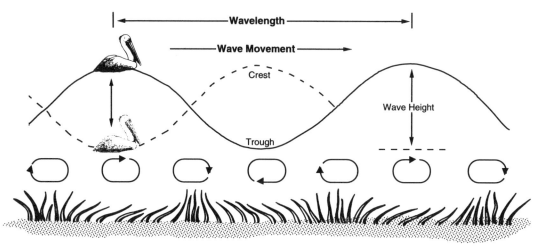

FIGURE 33: Oscillatory Wave ———— Surface Wave

- - - - Position of Previous Wave

Subsurface Water Movement

116

2. Translating waves are waves that transport water. This happens when waves break. See *breakers* and *surf zone* for explanations of how waves break and transport water as they approach the shore. Waves break in deeper water under a variety of conditions involving winds, currents, and overlapping waves which produce phenomena, such as standing waves, white caps, storm waves, and tidal waves (tsunamis).   [*breakers*]   [*surf zone*]

Wetland: a lowland whose water table is close to the surface of the ground forming sloughs, swamps, bogs, ponds, and freshwater marshes. A wetland is also a lowland that is inundated with tidal flow such as a salt marsh.

Wind shearing: the destruction of buds, limbs and leaves of trees through de-hydration from the wind. Wind shearing on the barrier islands is done by salt-laden sea breezes, so dehydration by salt (*salt pruning*) adds considerably to the desiccating effect of the wind. The windward limbs become more stunted than those on the more protected leeward side of the tree, allowing greater growth away from the direction of the prevailing winds. Forests near the beaches develop a backward-slanting shape to their canopies called a *shearline*. They often appear as if they were trimmed with a giant hedge clipper. With extreme windshearing of individual trees, such as the one illustrated at the bottom of the page, one becomes tempted to believe the common misconception that their lopsided features come from being stooped over by the force of the wind, rather than from differential growth.   [*shrubbing effect*]   (Site 2, page 66)

Wrack (tidal wrack): debris washed up along the high tide line of a beach. Dead cordgrass stalks make up a major portion of the tidal wrack on Georgia's beaches and contribute greatly to the growth of beaches.   (Ocean Beach, page 26).

APPENDICES

Clapper Rail

PLANT IDENTIFICATION

The plants are grouped as they appear in the various zones of each of the barrier island's ecosystems. Brief descriptions of identifying features for each plant and its flowering season are presented at the bottom of each page of illustrations. Where a plant equally inhabits other ecosystems besides the one in which it is illustrated, the other ecosystems are given in parentheses at the end of the identifying descriptions. In order to conserve space, the plant illustrations are not drawn to scale.

Ocean Beach

Upper Beach
(Pioneer plants)

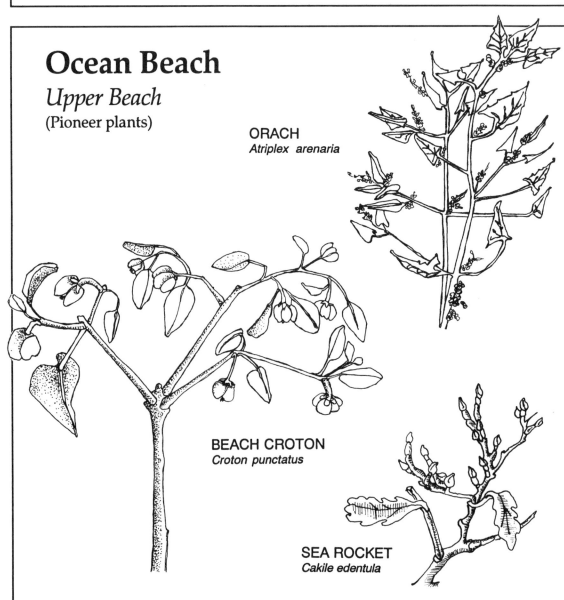

ORACH
Atriplex arenaria

BEACH CROTON
Croton punctatus

SEA ROCKET
Cakile edentula

ORACH: succulent gray-green leaf, red stem, summer.
BEACH CROTON: dusky gray-green leaves and stem, round fruit, spring.
SEA ROCKET: succulent plant, two-section fruit, dies in summer, spring.

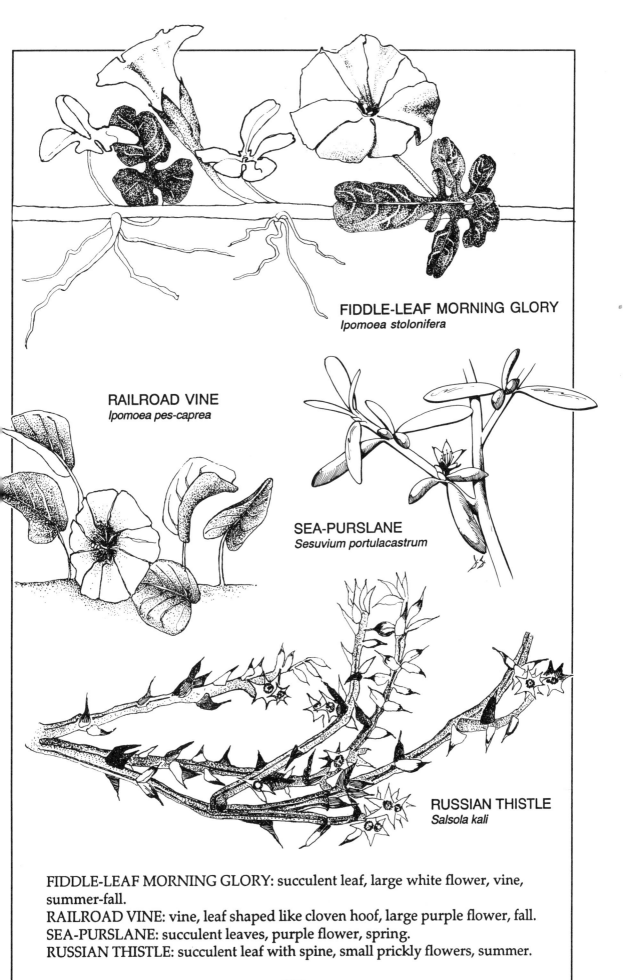

FIDDLE-LEAF MORNING GLORY
Ipomoea stolonifera

RAILROAD VINE
Ipomoea pes-caprea

SEA-PURSLANE
Sesuvium portulacastrum

RUSSIAN THISTLE
Salsola kali

FIDDLE-LEAF MORNING GLORY: succulent leaf, large white flower, vine, summer-fall.
RAILROAD VINE: vine, leaf shaped like cloven hoof, large purple flower, fall.
SEA-PURSLANE: succulent leaves, purple flower, spring.
RUSSIAN THISTLE: succulent leaf with spine, small prickly flowers, summer.

Primary Dunes

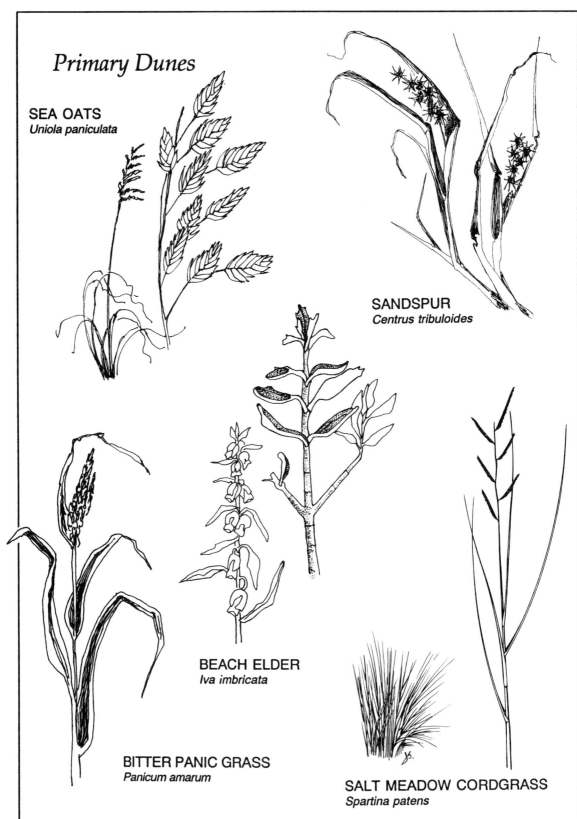

SEA OATS
Uniola paniculata

SANDSPUR
Centrus tribuloides

BEACH ELDER
Iva imbricata

BITTER PANIC GRASS
Panicum amarum

SALT MEADOW CORDGRASS
Spartina patens

SEA OATS: seed head on tall stalk, curly leaf blade, summer-fall.
SANDSPUR: prostrate, sharp painful burr, fall.
BEACH ELDER: succulent leaf, woody stem, summer.
BITTER PANIC GRASS: broad, alternate leaf blades on the stalk, summer.
SALT MEADOW CORDGRASS: narrow leaf blade, summer (saltmarsh).
DROPSEED GRASS: (not shown) similar to salt grass (see Salt Marsh).

Dune Meadows

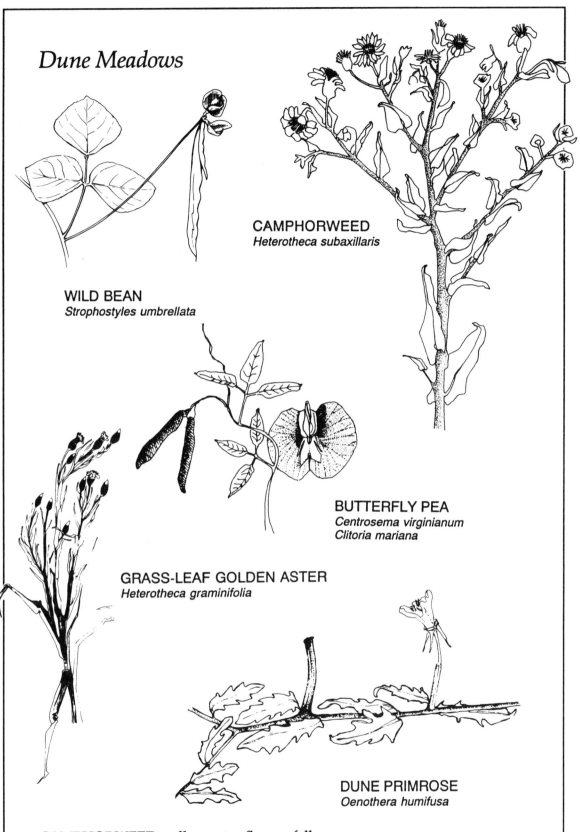

CAMPHORWEED
Heterotheca subaxillaris

WILD BEAN
Strophostyles umbrellata

BUTTERFLY PEA
Centrosema virginianum
Clitoria mariana

GRASS-LEAF GOLDEN ASTER
Heterotheca graminifolia

DUNE PRIMROSE
Oenothera humifusa

CAMPHORWEED: yellow aster flower, fall.
WILD BEAN: small red pea flower, slender black pod, vine, summer-fall.
BUTTERFLY PEA: large purple pea flower, vine, spring-fall (edge of woods).
GRASS-LEAF GOLDEN ASTER: yellow aster flower, grass-like leaf, summer.
DUNE PRIMROSE: prostrate, pink and yellow flower, spring-fall (fields).

Dune Meadows

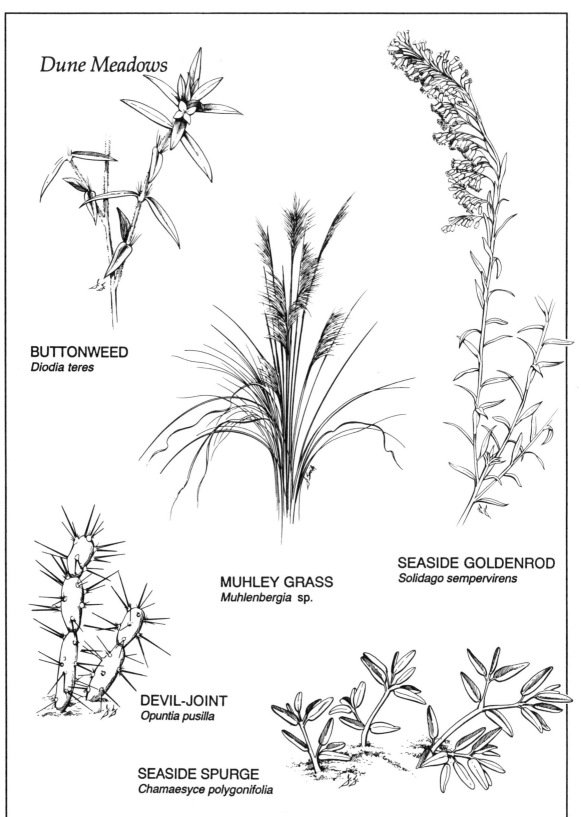

BUTTONWEED
Diodia teres

MUHLEY GRASS
Muhlenbergia sp.

SEASIDE GOLDENROD
Solidago sempervirens

DEVIL-JOINT
Opuntia pusilla

SEASIDE SPURGE
Chamaesyce polygonifolia

BUTTONWEED: prostrate, white four-petaled flower, summer-fall (fields).
SEASIDE GOLDENROD: tall, many golden flowers, fall (fields).
MUHLEY GRASS: many, tiny, lavender flowers on long, wispy panicles, fall
(fields and sloughs).
DEVIL-JOINT: small prickly-pear cactus, barbed spines, spring (fields).
SEASIDE SPURGE: small plant, opposite leaves, prostrate, summer.

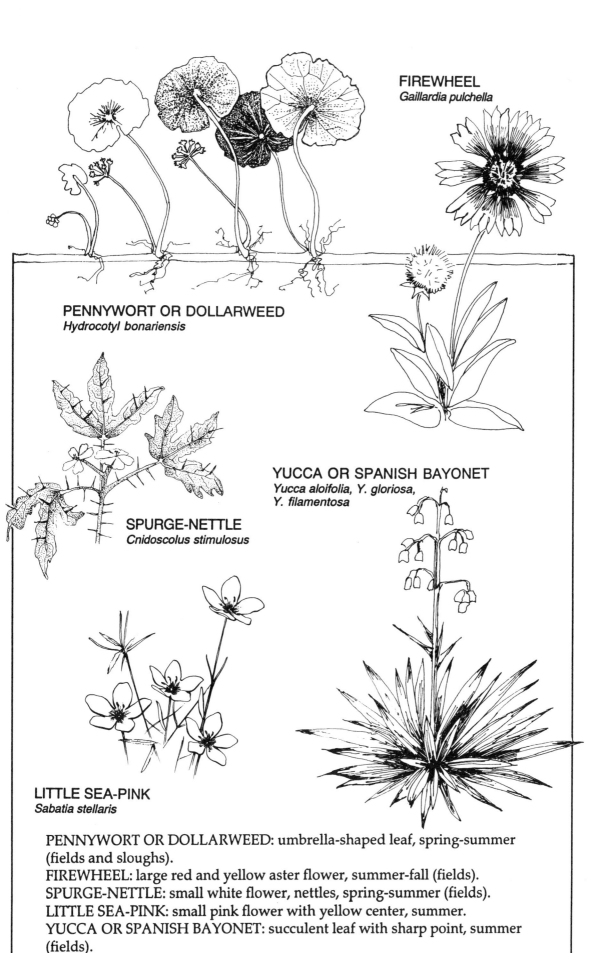

FIREWHEEL
Gaillardia pulchella

PENNYWORT OR DOLLARWEED
Hydrocotyl bonariensis

SPURGE-NETTLE
Cnidoscolus stimulosus

YUCCA OR SPANISH BAYONET
Yucca aloifolia, Y. gloriosa,
Y. filamentosa

LITTLE SEA-PINK
Sabatia stellaris

PENNYWORT OR DOLLARWEED: umbrella-shaped leaf, spring-summer
(fields and sloughs).
FIREWHEEL: large red and yellow aster flower, summer-fall (fields).
SPURGE-NETTLE: small white flower, nettles, spring-summer (fields).
LITTLE SEA-PINK: small pink flower with yellow center, summer.
YUCCA OR SPANISH BAYONET: succulent leaf with sharp point, summer
(fields).

125

Shrub Zone and Shrub Forest

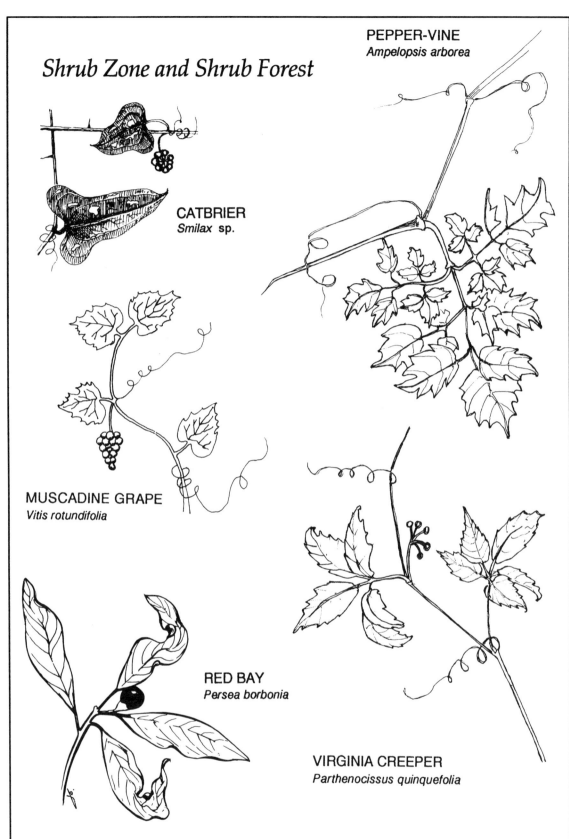

PEPPER-VINE
Ampelopsis arborea

CATBRIER
Smilax sp.

MUSCADINE GRAPE
Vitis rotundifolia

RED BAY
Persea borbonia

VIRGINIA CREEPER
Parthenocissus quinquefolia

CATBRIER OR GREENBRIER: thorns, black berry, shiny leaf, vine (woods).
PEPPER-VINE: black berry, leaf with many leaflets (fields).
MUSCADINE GRAPE: grapes, vine (woods).
RED BAY: aromatic leaf, tree (woods).
VIRGINIA CREEPER: leaf has five leaflets, vine (woods).

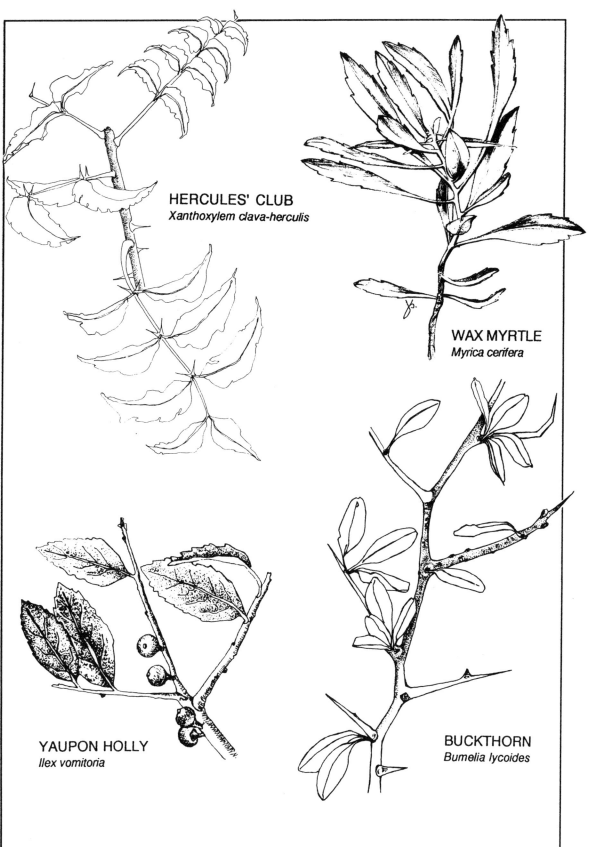

HERCULES' CLUB
Xanthoxylem clava-herculis

WAX MYRTLE
Myrica cerifera

YAUPON HOLLY
Ilex vomitoria

BUCKTHORN
Bumelia lycoides

HERCULES' CLUB: pointed warty growths on bark, thorns.
WAX MYRTLE: shrub, aromatic, clusters of small gray berries (woods).
YAUPON HOLLY: shrub, shiny evergreen leaf, red berry in winter, (woods).
BUCKTHORN: thorn often among whorls of leaves, small tree.

Salt Marsh
Low Marsh

SMOOTH CORDGRASS
Spartina alterniflora

SMOOTH CORDGRASS: broad leaf blade, plant size varies with salinity, fall.

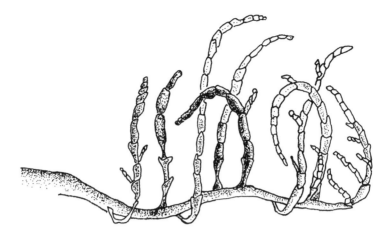

GLASSWORT
Salicornia virginica, S. bigelovii, S. europaea

SALT GRASS
Distichlis spicata

SALTWORT
Batis maritima

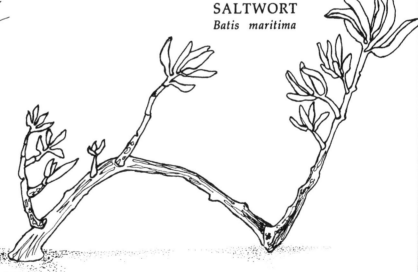

GLASSWORT OR PICKLE WEED: succulent plants with tiny
bract-like leaves.
SALT GRASS: leaf blades in one plane, summer-fall (beach meadows).
SALTWORT: succulent leaf, prostrate woody stem.

Marsh Border

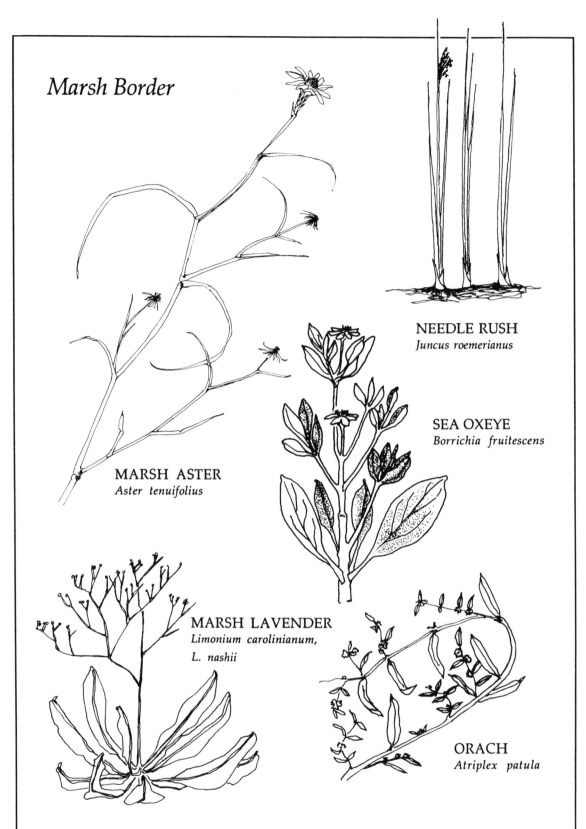

NEEDLE RUSH
Juncus roemerianus

SEA OXEYE
Borrichia fruitescens

MARSH ASTER
Aster tenuifolius

MARSH LAVENDER
Limonium carolinianum,
L. nashii

ORACH
Atriplex patula

MARSH ASTER: small sparsely-arranged lavender or white aster flowers with yellow centers, fall.
NEEDLE RUSH: long tubular leaves with sharp points, painful to walkers.
SEA OXEYE: succulent leaf, yellow aster flower, spiny burr, summer.
MARSH LAVENDER: small sparsely-arranged purple flowers, basal leaves, fall.
ORACH: similar to orach on beaches (A. arenaria) but smaller leaves.

Upper Marsh Border and Transition Zone

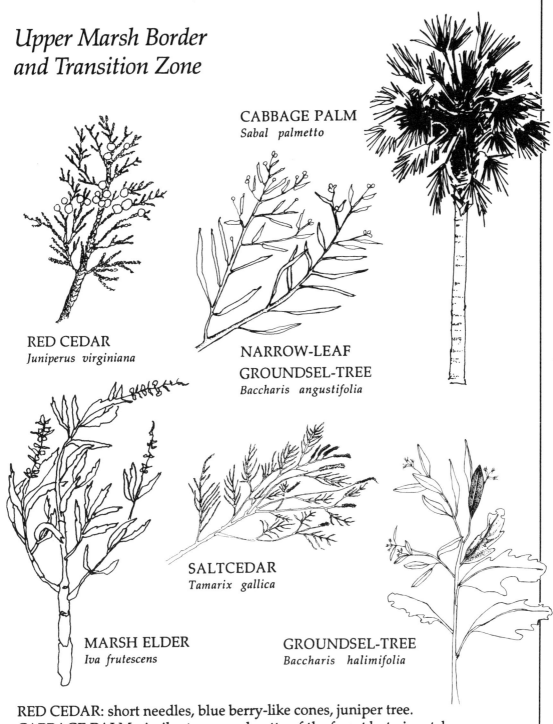

CABBAGE PALM
Sabal palmetto

RED CEDAR
Juniperus virginiana

NARROW-LEAF
GROUNDSEL-TREE
Baccharis angustifolia

SALTCEDAR
Tamarix gallica

MARSH ELDER
Iva frutescens

GROUNDSEL-TREE
Baccharis halimifolia

RED CEDAR: short needles, blue berry-like cones, juniper tree.
CABBAGE PALM: similar to saw palmetto of the forest but pinnately-arranged leaves and no spines on leaf stalks, tree.
NARROW-LEAF GROUNDSEL-TREE OR FALSE WILLOW: similar to groundsel-tree but rarer and with narrower leaves.
MARSH ELDER OR HIGH TIDE BUSH: serrated leaves, tiny flowers or seeds at end of stems, leaves not as fleshy as beach elder.
SALTCEDAR OR TAMARISK: small tree or shrub, similar to red cedar but paler green and more delicate, tiny pink flowers at tips of stems, summer.
GROUNDSEL-TREE OR COTTON BUSH: irregularly-shaped leaves, cotton-like seed tufts in the fall, shrub.

Freshwater Slough
Floating and Emergent Plants

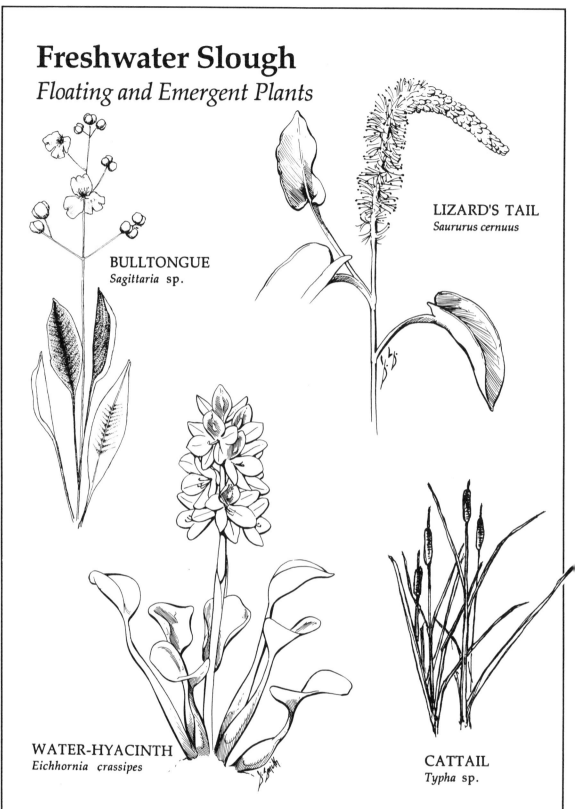

LIZARD'S TAIL
Saururus cernuus

BULLTONGUE
Sagittaria sp.

WATER-HYACINTH
Eichhornia crassipes

CATTAIL
Typha sp.

LIZARD'S TAIL: densely clustered, little white flowers on a spike, summer.
BULLTONGUE: sparsely-arranged white flowers on a spike, summer-fall.
CATTAIL: tall plants, narrow leaves, large brown hot dog-shaped flower heads, summer-fall.
WATER-HYACINTH: ornate blue flowers, inflated leaf bases, summer.

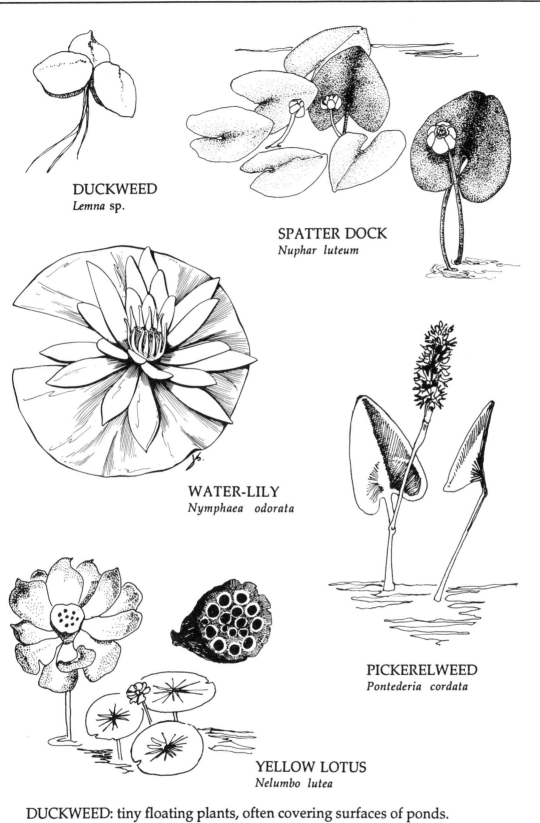

DUCKWEED
Lemna sp.

SPATTER DOCK
Nuphar luteum

WATER-LILY
Nymphaea odorata

PICKERELWEED
Pontederia cordata

YELLOW LOTUS
Nelumbo lutea

DUCKWEED: tiny floating plants, often covering surfaces of ponds.
SPATTER DOCK: yellow spherical flower, spring-fall.
WATER-LILY: large white or pink fragrant flower with yellow center, spring-summer.
PICKERELWEED: cylindrical blue flower head, summer-fall.
YELLOW LOTUS: yellow flower, large shower head-shaped seed pod, umbrella-shaped leaves, summer.

Wetland Plants

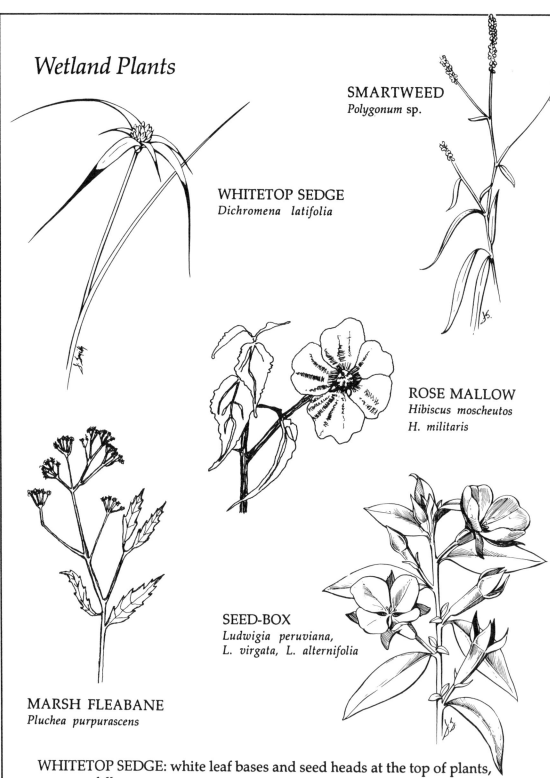

SMARTWEED
Polygonum sp.

WHITETOP SEDGE
Dichromena latifolia

ROSE MALLOW
Hibiscus moscheutos
H. militaris

SEED-BOX
Ludwigia peruviana,
L. virgata, L. alternifolia

MARSH FLEABANE
Pluchea purpurascens

WHITETOP SEDGE: white leaf bases and seed heads at the top of plants, summer-fall.

SMARTWEED: small spherical pink or white flowers on spikes, summer-fall.

ROSE MALLOW OR MARSH MALLOW: tall plant, large pink or white hibiscus flowers, summer-fall.

SEED-BOX: four-petaled yellow flowers, sizes of plants and flowers vary greatly with species, summer-fall.

MARSH FLEABANE OR CAMPHORWEED: heads of lavender aster flowers, summer-fall.

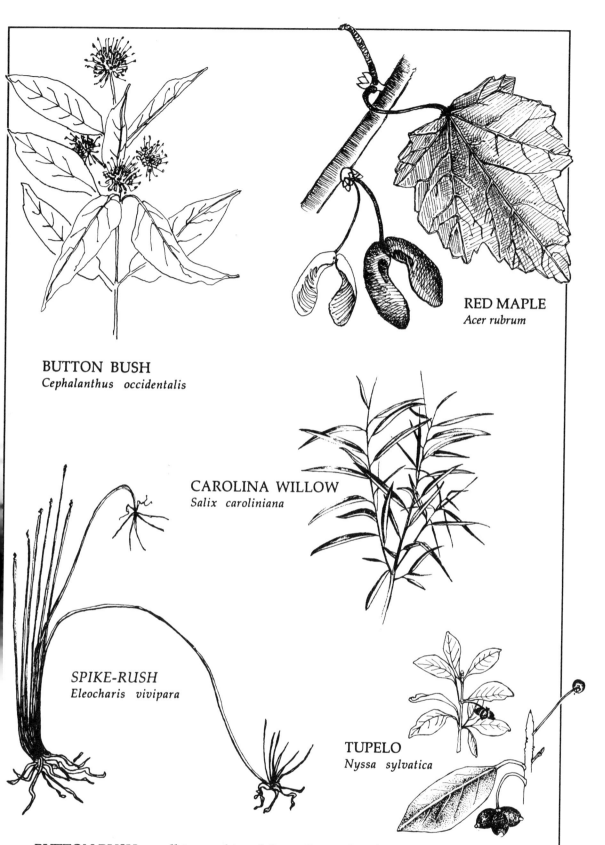

BUTTON BUSH
Cephalanthus occidentalis

RED MAPLE
Acer rubrum

CAROLINA WILLOW
Salix caroliniana

SPIKE-RUSH
Eleocharis vivipara

TUPELO
Nyssa sylvatica

BUTTON BUSH: small tree, white globose flower heads, summer-fall.
RED MAPLE: red leaf stalks, red winged fruits (forest).
CAROLINA WILLOW: a short-leaved willow on water-saturated soils.
SPIKE-RUSH: many species of delicate rushes with terminal seed heads.
This particular species has reclining stems with new shoots at stem tips.
TUPELO OR BLACKGUM: small elliptical leaf, small black berry.

135

Forest
Canopy

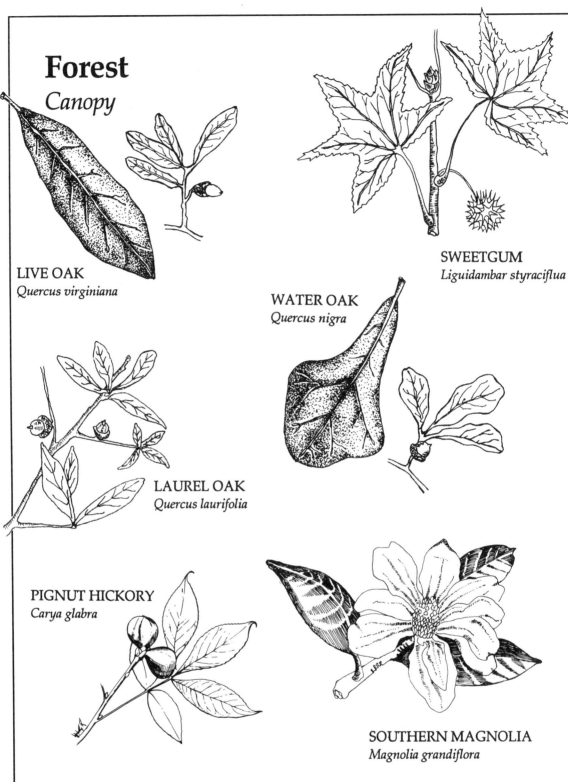

LIVE OAK
Quercus virginiana

SWEETGUM
Liguidambar styraciflua

WATER OAK
Quercus nigra

LAUREL OAK
Quercus laurifolia

PIGNUT HICKORY
Carya glabra

SOUTHERN MAGNOLIA
Magnolia grandiflora

LIVE OAK: leathery oblong leaf with margins slightly rolled downward, black narrow acorn.
SWEETGUM: five-pointed leaves, round spiny gum balls (wetlands).
WATER OAK: spatula-shaped leaf, stout yellow-brown acorn.
LAUREL OAK: narrow elliptical leaf, brown stout acorn.
PIGNUT HICKORY: leaf usually contains five leaflets, hard pear-shaped nut.
SOUTHERN MAGNOLIA: large shiny leaf with rust-colored underside, fruit with red seeds, huge white flowers, spring.

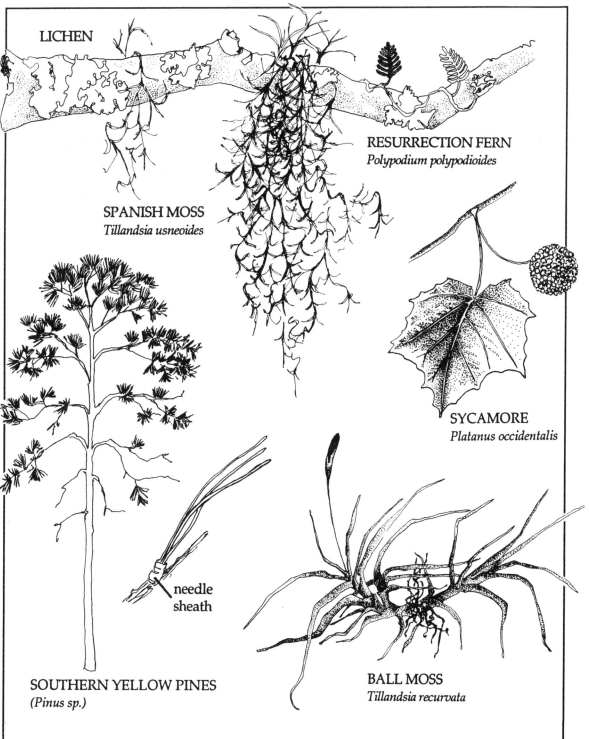

LICHEN

RESURRECTION FERN
Polypodium polypodioides

SPANISH MOSS
Tillandsia usneoides

SYCAMORE
Platanus occidentalis

needle
sheath

SOUTHERN YELLOW PINES
(Pinus sp.)

BALL MOSS
Tillandsia recurvata

EPIPHYTES: SPANISH MOSS, BALL MOSS, RESURRECTION FERN, LICHEN.
SYCAMORE: blotched bark, maple-like leaf, round many-faceted balls.
SOUTHERN YELLOW PINES (Pinus sp.):
    SLASH PINE (P. elliotti): mostly two needles per sheath, cones on short stalks, gray bark.
    LOBLOLLY (P. taeda): mostly three needles per sheath, cones with no stalks, reddish bark.
    LONG-LEAF (P. palustris): mostly three needles per sheath, needles and cones larger than the other pines.
    POND PINES (P. serotina): three to four needles per sheath, small cone.

Understory

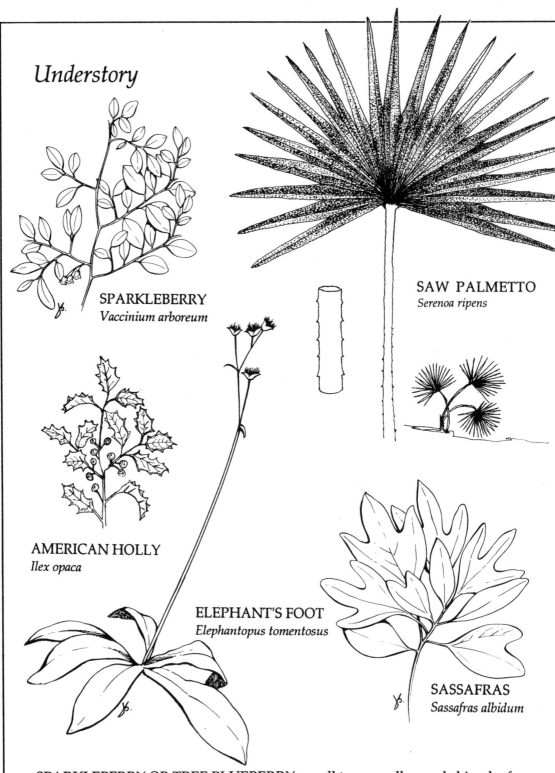

SPARKLEBERRY
Vaccinium arboreum

SAW PALMETTO
Serenoa ripens

AMERICAN HOLLY
Ilex opaca

ELEPHANT'S FOOT
Elephantopus tomentosus

SASSAFRAS
Sassafras albidum

SPARKLEBERRY OR TREE BLUEBERRY: small tree, small round shiny leaf, clusters of pink and white bell-shaped flowers, black berry, spring.
SAW PALMETTO: stems grow along the surface of ground, saw-toothed margins on leaf stalks, leaflets grow out from center (palmate), shrub.
AMERICAN HOLLY: small to middle-sized tree, spiny leaf, red berries.
ELEPHANT'S FOOT: rosette of hairy basal leaves, small cluster of modest purple flowers at the end of a long stalk, summer-fall.
SASSAFRAS: small tree, irregularly-lobed leaf (often mitten-shaped), distinct odor.

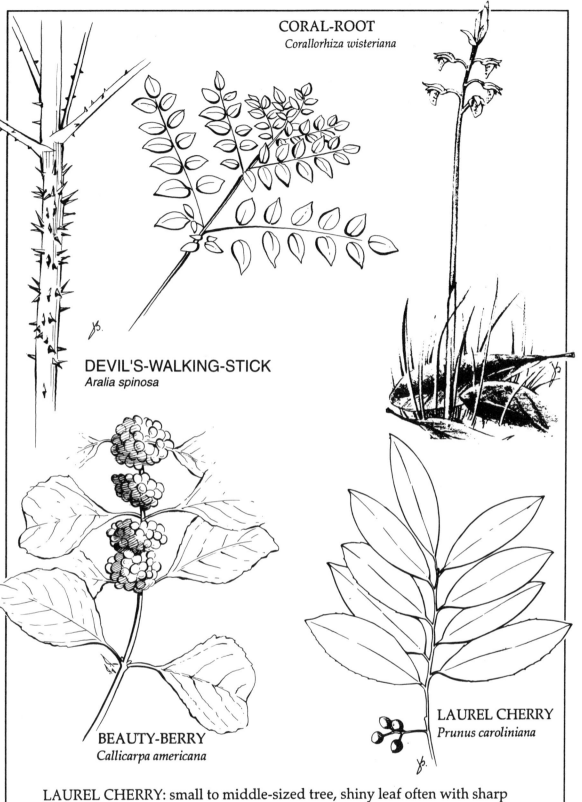

CORAL-ROOT
Corallorhiza wisteriana

DEVIL'S-WALKING-STICK
Aralia spinosa

BEAUTY-BERRY
Callicarpa americana

LAUREL CHERRY
Prunus caroliniana

LAUREL CHERRY: small to middle-sized tree, shiny leaf often with sharp
small points on leaf margin, black berry.
CORAL-ROOT: rust-colored orchid consisting of a stalk bearing a few small
flowers, no leaves, found in leaf-litter under oaks, spring.
BEAUTY-BERRY: shrub, spherical clusters of purple-magenta flowers and
berries at the leaf axes, spring.
DEVIL'S-WALKING-STICK: whorles of thorns, long branching
leaves with many leaflets, fall

139

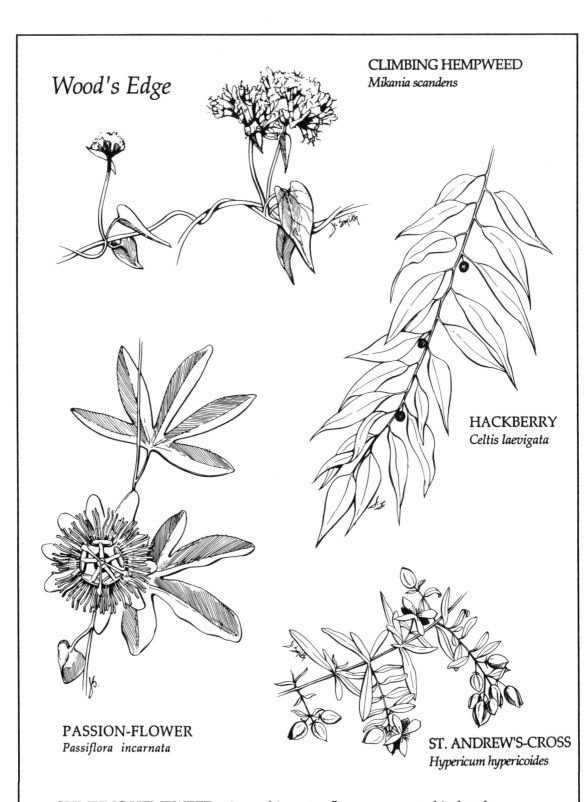

Wood's Edge

CLIMBING HEMPWEED
Mikania scandens

HACKBERRY
Celtis laevigata

PASSION-FLOWER
Passiflora incarnata

ST. ANDREW'S-CROSS
Hypericum hypericoides

CLIMBING HEMPWEED: vine, white aster flowers arranged in heads, summer-fall (fields).
HACKBERRY: shrub or tree, leaves alternate and arranged in one plane, small red-brown fruit, bark ash-gray often with spiny growths (fields).
PASSION-FLOWER OR MAYPOP: vine, distinctive complex blue flowers, green passion fruit, summer-fall.
ST. ANDREW'S-CROSS: narrow four-petaled flower, disk-shaped pod, summer-fall (fields).

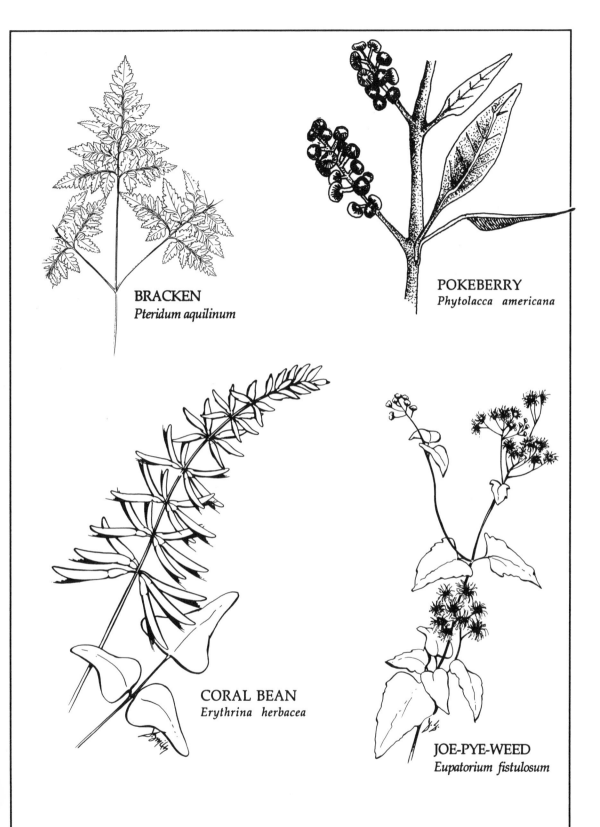

BRACKEN
Pteridum aquilinum

POKEBERRY
Phytolacca americana

CORAL BEAN
Erythrina herbacea

JOE-PYE-WEED
Eupatorium fistulosum

BRACKEN: medium-sized brittle fern, three-branched leaves (fields).
POKEBERRY: large leafy weed, clusters of black berries (fields).
CORAL BEAN: leaves having three pear-shaped leaflets, spikes of elongated red flowers, spring-summer (fields).
JOE-PYE-WEED: stems and leaves wooly, purple flower heads, fall (sloughs, fields).

141

Fields and Roadsides

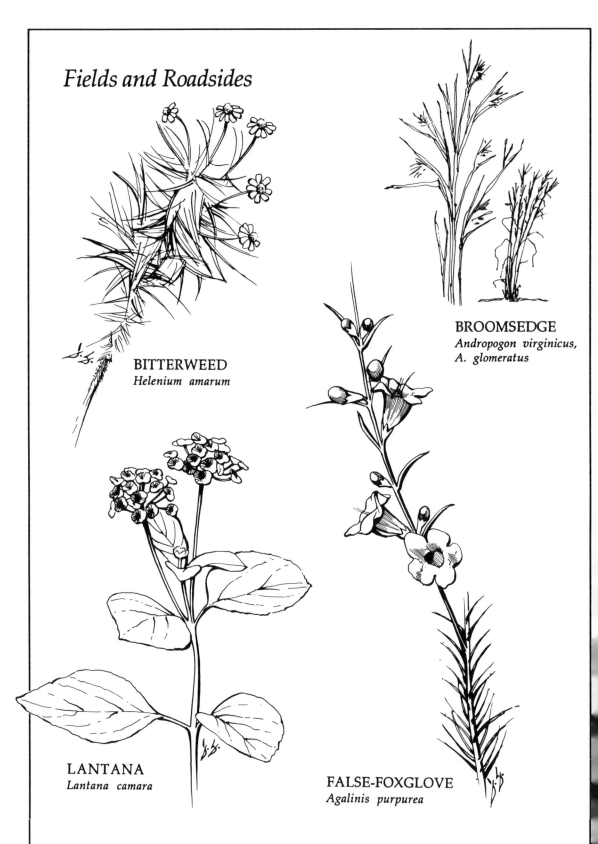

BITTERWEED
Helenium amarum

BROOMSEDGE
Andropogon virginicus,
A. glomeratus

LANTANA
Lantana camara

FALSE-FOXGLOVE
Agalinis purpurea

BITTERWEED: small bushy weed, yellow aster flowers, bitter taste, summer.
BROOMSEDGE: rust-colored grass, white seed tufts in fall.
LANTANA: shrub, yellow and orange (or pink) flowers on heads, summer-fall.
FALSE-FOXGLOVE OR GERARDIA: purple to pink trumpet-shaped flowers.
Flowers grow at leaf axes throughout the length of the branch, fall.

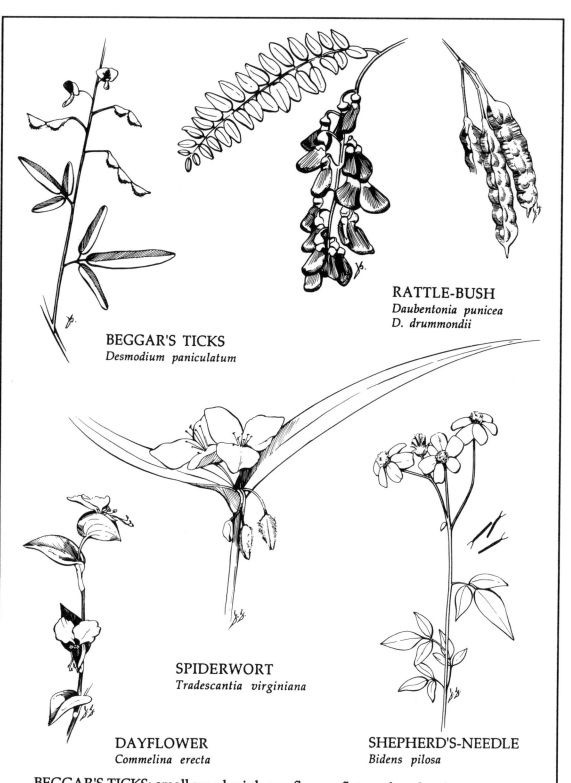

RATTLE-BUSH
Daubentonia punicea
D. drummondii

BEGGAR'S TICKS
Desmodium paniculatum

SPIDERWORT
Tradescantia virginiana

DAYFLOWER
Commelina erecta

SHEPHERD'S-NEEDLE
Bidens pilosa

BEGGAR'S TICKS: small weed, pink pea flower, flat seed pods whose triangular segments easily break off and stick to clothing, summer-fall.
RATTLE-BUSH: *D. punicea* has orange-red pea flowers, *D. drummondii* has yellow flowers, both have winged pods, summer-fall.
SPIDERWORT: clusters of blue three-petaled flowers, spring-summer.
DAYFLOWER: flowers with two blue petals and third greatly reduced, summer.
SHEPHERD'S-NEEDLE: white aster flower with yellow center, barbed needle-like seeds which stick to clothing, all year.

143

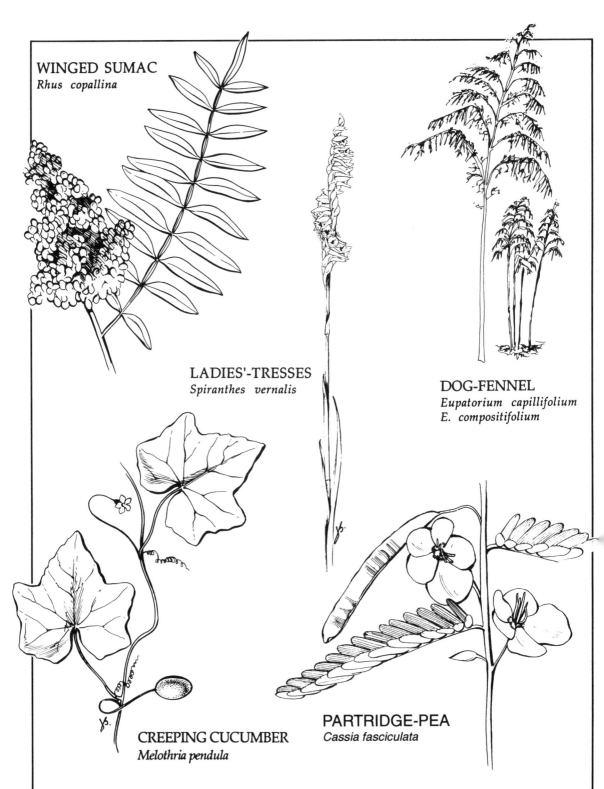

WINGED SUMAC
Rhus copallina

LADIES'-TRESSES
Spiranthes vernalis

DOG-FENNEL
Eupatorium capillifolium
E. compositifolium

CREEPING CUCUMBER
Melothria pendula

PARTRIDGE-PEA
Cassia fasciculata

WINGED SUMAC: shrub, narrow wings on leaf stems, clusters of dull-red flowers, fall.

DOG-FENNEL: tall weed, many small white flowers on pointed heads at the top of branches, fall.

CREEPING CUCUMBER: vine, small three-lobed leaf, small yellow flower, miniature cucumber (poisonous), summer-fall.

LADIES' TRESSES: orchid, small spirally-arranged white flowers, spring.

PARTRIDGE-PEA: yellow flowers with red centers, fall (beach meadow)

ANIMAL IDENTIFICATION

The animals identified in this section are limited to commonly-seen invertebrates living on ocean beaches and salt marshes and in their nearshore waters. There are excellent field guides which cover other animal phyla, and identify seashells and other animal remains washed up onto the beach. Brief descriptons of the invertebrate, its burrow or other evidence of its presence are given at the bottom of each page. Where an invertebrate is commonly found in an ecosystem other than the one designated, the other appears in parentheses at the end of the description. The animal illustrations are not drawn to scale.

Ocean Beach

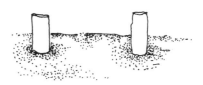

ONUPHIS WORM burrows
Onuphis sp.

POLYCHAETE WORM

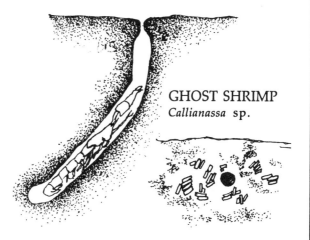

GHOST SHRIMP
Callianassa sp.

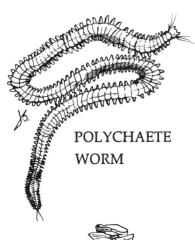

PLUMED WORM burrow
Diapatra cuprea

GHOST SHRIMP burrow with fecal pellets

POLYCHAETE WORM: many species varying in size and appearance on shore and in aquatic environments.
ONUPHIS WORM: parchment-like burrow entrance, in low tide zone, the polychaete rarely seen.
PLUMED WORM: burrow entrance with shell and plant fragments attached, in low tide zone, the polychaete rarely seen.
GHOST SHRIMP: burrow often surrounded by small fecal pellets, in low tide zone, animal 3-to 5-inch-long white-pinkish body, the animal rarely seen (marsh).

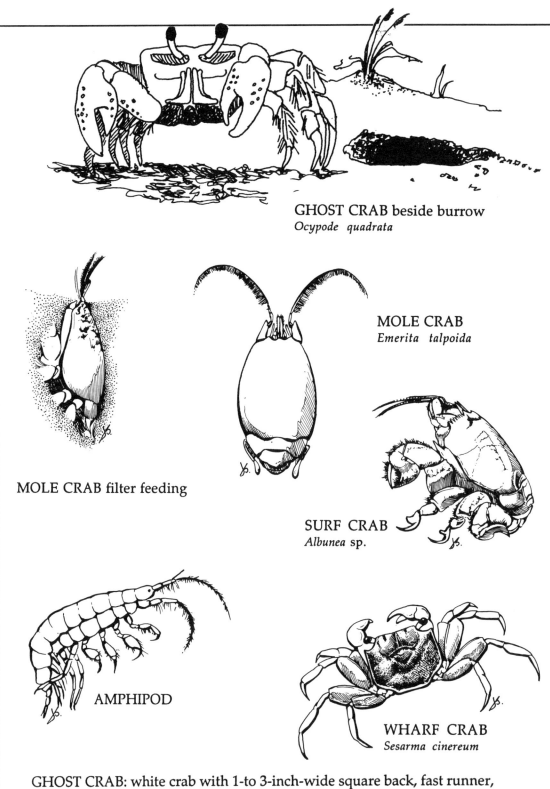

GHOST CRAB beside burrow
Ocypode quadrata

MOLE CRAB
Emerita talpoida

MOLE CRAB filter feeding

SURF CRAB
Albunea sp.

AMPHIPOD

WHARF CRAB
Sesarma cinereum

GHOST CRAB: white crab with 1-to 3-inch-wide square back, fast runner, more commonly seen at night, burrow in upper beach.
MOLE CRAB: 1-inch-long egg-shaped white crab, seen just below surface of sand in the swash zone, in the northern and southern regions.
SURF CRAB OR MOLE CRAB: stouter and shaped differently than the other mole crab and found in same habitat, southern species.
AMPHIPOD: many species in shore and aquatic environments.
WHARF CRAB: 1/2-inch brown square-backed crab, often found among tidal wrack (marsh).

LETTERED OLIVE
Oliva sayana

MOON SNAIL
Polinices duplicatus

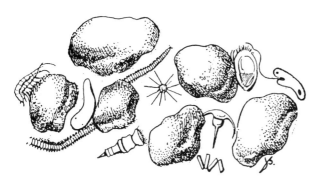

COQUINA CLAM
Donax sp.

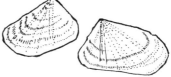

PSAMMON

SAND DOLLAR
Mellita quinquiesperforata

LETTERED OLIVE: elongated glassy-smooth shell with V-shaped markings, crawls just under the surface of sand leaving convoluted trails visible in the low tide zone, feeds on coquina clams.

MOON SNAIL: almost spherical shell with large opening, leaves trails similar to the lettered olive in low tide zone, makes small beveled holes in bivalve and other moon snail shells to feeding.

PSAMMON: tiny plants and animals which live among the sand grains.

COQUINA CLAM: small, roughly triangular shell of varying colors, found in the surf zone.

SAND DOLLAR: brown flat urchin with short bristle-like spines, five openings in shell, seen just below surface of sand in shallow water.

Salt Marsh
Molluscs

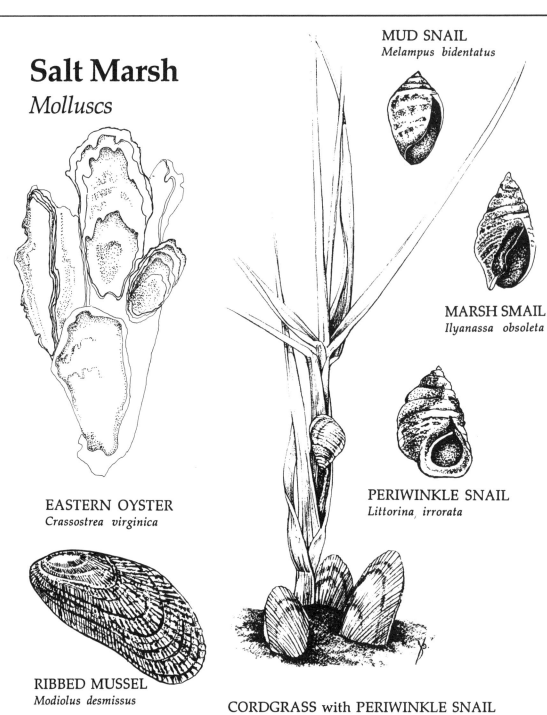

MUD SNAIL
Melampus bidentatus

MARSH SMAIL
Ilyanassa obsoleta

PERIWINKLE SNAIL
Littorina, irrorata

EASTERN OYSTER
Crassostrea virginica

RIBBED MUSSEL
Modiolus desmissus

CORDGRASS with PERIWINKLE SNAIL on stem, RIBBED MUSSELS at base.

OYSTERS: gray irregularly-shaped shell, often found in clusters attached to root masses or other firm surfaces (rocks on beach).

RIBBED MUSSEL: gray to brown shell, attached to cordgrass or other firm surfaces by bysasus threads, usually partially buried in mud (rocks on beach).

MUD SNAIL OR COFFEE-BEAN SNAIL: 1/2-inch-long black shell, often found close to plants or detritus near the high tide line.

MARSH SNAIL:1-inch-long black shell, shell often partially corroded, thousands often seen on tidal flats.

PERIWINKLE SNAIL: white snail found on cordgrass stalks.

Crabs

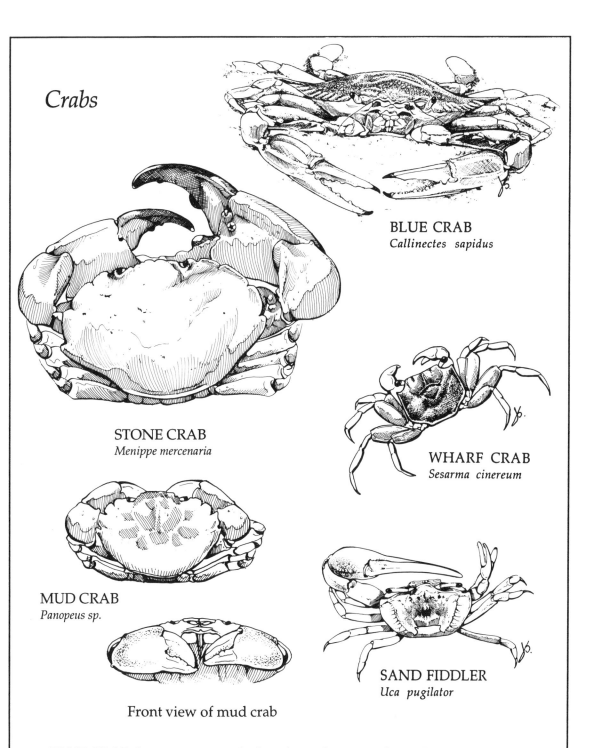

BLUE CRAB
Callinectes sapidus

STONE CRAB
Menippe mercenaria

WHARF CRAB
Sesarma cinereum

MUD CRAB
Panopeus sp.

SAND FIDDLER
Uca pugilator

Front view of mud crab

BLUE CRAB: large aquatic crab that abounds in marsh creeks, sounds and shallow offshore waters, green to brown shell, blue on claws, edible.
WHARF CRAB: 1- to 2-inch, flat, brown square-backed crab. The MARSH CRAB (S. reticulatum) is similar but black and stouter (not shown).
MUD CRABS: many species of middle sized crabs with oval shells and stout claws. The STONE CRAB is the giant of this group, claws edible.
FIDDLER CRABS: (Ulca sp.)
   SAND FIDDLER (U. pugilator): purple on back, white claw.
   MUD FIDDLER (U. pugnax): brown body, blue line above eyes, yellow claw.
   BRACKLISH-WATER FIDDLER (U. minax): larger than the other fiddlers, black back paler towards face, red dots on claw joints, white claw.

149

Plankton

PHYTOPLANKTON

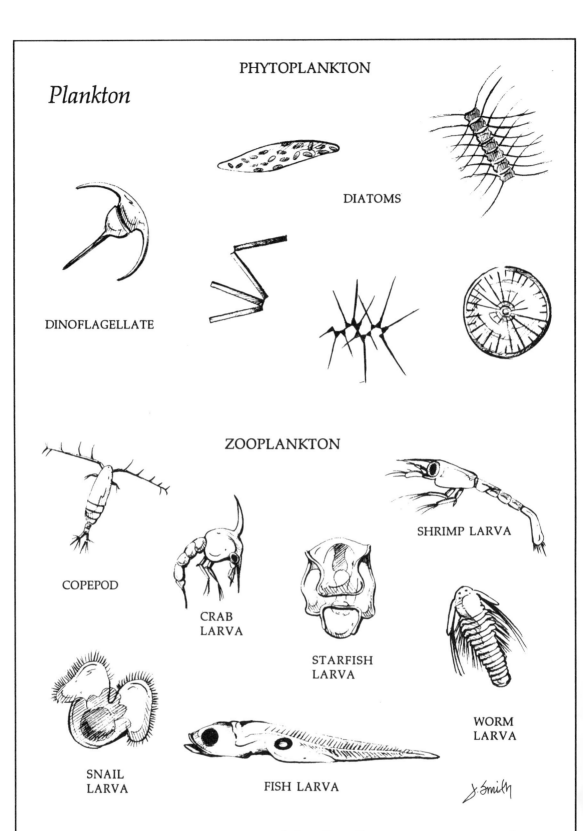

DIATOMS

DINOFLAGELLATE

ZOOPLANKTON

SHRIMP LARVA

COPEPOD

CRAB
LARVA

STARFISH
LARVA

WORM
LARVA

SNAIL
LARVA

FISH LARVA

J. Smith

PHYTOPLANKTON: Diatoms and dinoflagellates are microscopic algae and are a major producer for the animals of the salt marsh and ocean. ZOOPLANKTON: The microscopic copepods and the larval stages of many of the animals of the salt marsh are the major consumers of phytoplankton and smaller zooplankton. These provide a vital food source for the animals growing in these nursery grounds.

SUGGESTED READING

1. *Life and Death of a Salt Marsh,* John and Mildred Teal, Ballantine Books.

2. *Seasons of the Salt Marsh,* David Allen Gates, Chatham Press.

3. *Portrait of an Island,* John and Mildred Teal, Univ. of Georgia Press.

4. *Sea Islands of Georgia,* Count D. Gibson, Univ. of Georgia Press.

5. *Tideland Treasures,* Todd Ballantine, Deerfield Publishing, Inc.

6. *The Edge of the Sea,* Rachel Carson, Houghton Mifflin, Co.

7. *Living with the Georgia Shore,* Tonya D. Clayton *et al.,* Duke Univ. Press.

8. *Beaches Are Moving,* W. Kaufman and Orrin Pilkey, Anchor Press.

9. *A Naturalist's Guide to St. Simons Island,* Taylor Schoettle, Watermarks Publishing.

10. *St. Simons Island, a summary of its history,* Edwin Green, Arner Publications. (Under new title: *History and Mystery of St. Simons*).

11. *Historic Glimpses of St. Simons Island, 1736-1924,* The Coastal Georgia Historical Society, St. Simons Island, Ga.

12. *A Graphic History of St. Simons Island,* Tommy Jenkins, Watermarks Publishing.

13. *Georgia's Land of the Golden Isles,* B. Vanstory, Univ. of Georgia Press.

14. *Early Days on the Georgia Tidewater: the Story of McIntosh County and Sapelo,* Buddy Sullivan, McIntosh County Board of Commissioners.

FIELD GUIDES AND HANDBOOKS:

1. *Seashore Animals of the Southeast,* Edward Ruppert and Richard Fox, Univ. of South Carolina Press.

2. *A Field Guide to the Atlantic Seashore,* Kenneth Gosner, Houghton Mifflin, Co.

3. *The Erotic Ocean,* Jack Rudloe, E. P. Dutton, Inc.

4. *A Guide to Field Identification: Seashells of North America,* Tucker Abbott, Golden Press.

5. *Beachcomber's Guide to the Golden Isles*, Fr. Bertrand Dunegan, O.S.B., Benedictine Priory, Sanannah, Ga.

6. *1001 Questions Answered about the Seashore*, N. Berrill and J. Berrill, Dover Publications, Inc.

7. *Wildflowers of the Southeastern United States*, Wilber Duncan and Leonard Foote, Univ. of Georgia Press.

8. *Seaside Plants of the Gulf and Atlantic Coasts*, Wilber and Marion Duncan, Smithsonian Institution Press.

9. *Trees of the Southeastern United States*, Wilber and Marion Duncan, Wormsloe Foundation Publications.

10. *Native Flora of the Golden Isles*, Gladys Fendig and Esther Stewart, produced in St. Simons Island, Ga.

11. *A Guide to the Georgia Coast*, Georgia Conservancy, Miller Press.

12. *A Field Guide to the Birds*, Roger Peterson, Houghton Mifflin Co.

13. *Birds of North America*, Chandler Robbins *et al.*, Golden Press.

APPENDIX D

BIBLIOGRAPHY

1. Fox, W. T. 1983. *At the Sea's Edge.* Prentice Hall Press, New York, N.Y., p. 43.

2. Richards, H.G. 1968. "Illustrated Fossils of the Georgia Coastal Plain." Reprinted by the Georgia Dept. of Mines, Mining and Geology from Richards' articles in the Georgia Mineral Newsletter, Academy of Natural Sciences, Philadelphia, Pa.

3. Hoyt, J. H. 1968. "Geology of the Golden Isles and Lower Georgia Coastal Plain." Conference on the Future of the Marshlands and Islands of Georgia, p. 26.

4. Henry, V. J. 1987. "Updates on the Geology of the Georgia Coast." Lecture, Jekyll Island, Ga.

5. Titus, J. G. 1988. "Sea Level Rise and Wetland Loss: an Overview." Office of Policy Analysis, United States Environmental Protection Agency, Government Printing Office, Washington, D.C.

6. Schoettle, H. E. T. 1993. *Naturalist's Guide to St. Simons Island.* Watermarks Publishing, St. Simons Island, Ga.

7. Kaufmann, W. and O. H. Pilkey. 1979. *Beaches Are Moving.* Anchor Press, Doubleday, New York, N.Y.

8. Schoettle, H. E. T. 1985. *Field Guide to Sea Island.* University of Georgia Printing Dept., Sea Island Company, Sea Island, Ga.

9. Teal, J. and M. Teal. 1969. *Life and Death of the Salt Marsh.* Ballantine Books, New York, N.Y.

10. Rudlow, J. 1979. *Time of the Turtle.* Penguin Books Ltd., New York, N.Y.

11. Koske, R. E. and W. R. Polson. 1984. "Are VA Mycorrhizae Required for Sand Dune Stabilization?" BioScience, Vol. 34, No. 7, p. 420-422.

12. Stevens, E. L. 1931. "How Old Are the Live Oaks?" Am. Forests, Vol. 37.

13. Coder, K. D. 1989. "Live Oak, State Tree of Georgia," University of Georgia Cooperative Extension Service Publication, #309.

14. "Columbus and the Land of Ayllon." Sept.,1992, Seminar, Darien, Ga.

15. Green, R. E. 1989. *St. Simons Island: a Brief Summary of Its History.* Arner Publications, Rome, N.Y.

16. Coggins, J. 1969. *Ships and Seamen of the American Revolution.* Stackpole Books, Harrisburg, Pa.

17. Wood, V. S. 1981. *Live Oaking: Southern Timber for Tall Ships*, Northeastern Univ. Press, Boston, Ma.

18. Sullivan, B. 1992. *Early Days on the Georgia Tidewater,* 3rd ed. McIntosh County Board of Commissioners, Darien, Ga.

19. Cate, M. D. 1963. "Gascoigne Bluff." Reprinted from "American Neptune," Vol. 23, No. 2 by Ft. Frederica Association, St. Simons Island, Ga., p. 14.

20. McCash, W. B. and J. H. McCash 1989. *The Jekyll Island Club.* University of Georgia Press, Athens, Ga.

21. Schoettle, H. E. T. 1983. *Field Guide to Jekyll Island* (2nd ed. in 1987), University of Georgia Printing Dept., Sea Grant College Program, Athens, Ga.

22. Rathburn, R. R. July 1995. Director of the Jekyll Island Museum and Historic Restoration for the Jekyll Island Authority. Personal communication.

23. United States Coastal Survey Map of Jekyll Island. 1889. New York, N.Y.

24. Olson Associates, Inc. "Feasibility Study of Glynn County, Georgia Beach Restoration," Executive Report, 1988. p. 22.

25. National Research Council 1990. *Decline of the Sea Turtles: Causes and Prevention.* National Academy Press, Washington D.C.

26. Bascom, W. 1980. *Waves and Beaches.* Anchor Books, New York, p. 216-222.

27. Fritz, W. J. and J. N. Moore 1988. *Basics of Physical Stratigraphy and Sedimentology.* John Wiley & Sons, Inc, New York.

28. Duncan, W. H. 1985. Professor of Botany, University of Georgia. Personal communication.

APPENDIX E
PERSONAL SAFETY

EXPOSURE TO SUN

Some kind of protection from sunburn is needed all the seasons of the year. The reflected light from water and sand, and strong breezes intensify sunburn. A hat is recommended to keep from burning the head, bridge of the nose and cheeks and to help ward off sand gnats from the scalp, their favorite area of attack.

CLOTHING

Old shoes or sneakers should be worn in the marshes and woods. Bring extra clothing and shoes; temperature changes in autumn, winter, and spring are often quite sudden. Having a change of clothes and shoes is a blessing after slipping on the mud, falling in the water, or having to slog through the surf because of an unplanned tide change.

BUGS

Blood-sucking insects can make life miserable. Be sure to carry insect repellent with you on your excursions. Repellents, such as Off, Cutter or Repel, are good for mosquitos, biting flies, ticks, and chiggers (red bugs). Avon's Skin-So-Soft is best against sand gnats. There are various times and seasons when mosquitos, sand gnats and biting flies are out in force. During the middle hours of the day, mosquitos and sand gnats are usually not the problem they are during dusk and dawn, so you may not need to apply repellents in open areas, such as the beach and marsh until it becomes necessary.

If you are going to walk in the woods, a cursory spray with an insect repellent on the ankles, bottom of trouser legs, sleeves, waist line and collar helps to ward off ticks and chiggers. A tick check on the exposed body and clothes is well advised after a walk and later when removing clothes. Keep an eye out for both the large and the tiny ticks. (Incidences of Lymes disease carried by the tiny deer tick occasionally occur on this coast.) Be careful of fire ant nests in beach meadows, forest edges, road sides, and other areas with dry, sandy soils.

DRINKING WATER AND HEAT

The heat of summer, especially with the high humidity, is intense. Coupled with the sun and wind, excessive dehydration and heat exhaustion can easily occur especially on longer field trips. Carrying water on your person is a good idea and is imperative on longer field trips. If oppressive heat and breathless conditions are encountered at a particular site, limit the length of your stay, and perhaps return at a cooler time. Such oppressive conditions often occur in sun-drenched areas that are blocked from the breezes.

Always keep in touch with how you are feeling in the heat. Dizziness, nausea or shortness of breath, profuse sweating, and redness of face are signs of impending heat exhaustion. If you are experiencing any of these symptoms, find a shady place (if possible with a breeze) and mop water on the head, neck, insides of forearms and wrists to cool the blood in those vascularized areas, and rest in the shade until you feel better. If on a beach, a dunk in the ocean greatly helps -- I have done this many times.

SNAKES

Two kinds of rattlesnakes (eastern diamondback and pygmy rattler) and the cottonmouth moccasin are the most commonly found vipers on barrier islands. Rattlers can be found in almost any environment but prefer shaded places with lots of cover, such as shrub-thickets, palmetto fronds, dead branches and other forest-litter and trash piles. Cottonmouths tend to stay in and around freshwater sloughs. Although encountering these snakes is rare, caution and common sense are advised. Be careful not to walk in places that you cannot see where you are stepping. If you must step over a fallen tree, be sure to clear the other side by a broad margin -- a snake could be sitting under the log. If you encounter a snake, leave it alone and it will leave you alone. Most accounts of snake bite occur from people "fooling" with them.

GENERAL FIRST AID

Ammonia water or alcohol helps ease jellyfish and insect stings. Antiseptic ointments or tinctures and a can of assorted band-aids and gauze pads should be sufficient for cuts and scratches incurred from thorny vines, thistles, sand spurs and cactus, as well as from cuts on the feet from shells or other sharp objects in the water. Headaches can result from long exposure to sun, heat and glare, so aspirin, Tylenol, ibuprofen, or some other analgesic should be among your first aid supplies.

About the Author

Taylor was born in Philadelphia. After receiving BS and MS degrees in physiology and zoology, he taught high school biology for 12 years. Over those years he amassed a fine collection of snakes and birds with which he gave lectures in the Philadelphia area, and which eventually led to a zoo career. Taylor was curator for three zoos: in Puerto Rico, Oklahoma City and El Paso. In El Paso, Taylor was greatly moved by the scenes of the movie "Conrack", a great part of which was filmed on St. Simons. This impression was instrumental in the Schoettle family eventually moving to St. Simons Island.

In 1979 Taylor became a Marine Education Specialist with the University of Georgia Marine Extension Service in Brunswick. For the next two years, while offering a wide range of marine and coastal education programs, he became aware that his programs were not sufficient to meet the range and quantity of the interest groups. The need spawned the writing of three field guides and the other publications listed on the opposite page.

In 1982, a docent program was conceived by Taylor to help meet the interests of the residents and visitors to the coast. To date, the docents have reached over 100 thousand people through a variety of regularly scheduled nature walks and boat rides on Jekyll, St. Simons and Sea Islands. They also conduct classes, and walks for Elderhostels and school groups.

To meet the increasing demand of school groups from Georgia and neighboring states, Taylor conceived, with the University of Georgia 4-H Program, the Jekyll Island Environmental Education Center which today houses and instructs more than 20 thousand students and teachers each year. Later, he assisted in the development of two other centers on Tybee Island, Savannah and at Honey Creek, Dover Bluff.

Now independent, Taylor conducts lecture and field programs for college and school groups, summer teacher programs, natural history societies, Elderhostels, and conferences. He trains interpretive staff and produces educational materials for environmental education centers. Between appointments, Taylor continues to produce publications on coastal topics, and to compose songs about the coast, environmental ethics, and God.

List of Publications

A Field Guide to Jekyll Island. Georgia Sea Grant College Program, University of Georgia, Athens, Ga.

A Field Guide to Sea Island. Georgia Sea Grant College Program and The Sea Island Co., Sea Island, Ga.

A Naturalist's Guide to St. Simons Island. Watermarks Publishing and Printing, St. Simons Island, Ga.

A Guide to a Georgia Barrier Island. Watermarks Publishing and Printing, St. Simons Island, Ga.

"The Blue Crab" (videotape). Georgia Sea Grant College Program, University of Georgia Marine Extension Service, Brunswick, Ga.

A Study Approach to the Georgia Coast: Unit 1, The Ocean Beach; Unit 2, A Profile of a Salt Marsh; Unit 3, Organisms of the Dock, Georgia Sea Grant Program, University of Georgia, Athens, Ga.

The old schoolhouse from the movie, "Conrack,"
The movie that changed my journey's tack,
To bring me here to this special place,
To live my days in the Isles' embrace.

The schoolhouse sat abandoned in a field
And wild things dwelled beneath its shield.
Long since fallen through time and decay
Now only a memory that brought me this way.

Notes

Notes